Romantic Kentucky

More Than 300 Things to do for Southern Lovers

Leila W. Salisbury

Laura E. Sutton

John F. Blair Publisher   Winston-Salem, North Carolina

Published by John F. Blair, Publisher

The paper in this book meets the guidelines
for permanence and durability of the
Committee on Production Guidelines for
Book Longevity of the Council on Library Resources.

Library of Congress Cataloging-in-Publication Data

Salisbury, Leila W.
Romantic Kentucky : more than 300 things to do for southern lovers / Leila W.
Salisbury, Laura E. Sutton.
p.   cm.
Includes bibliographical references (p.   ) and index.
ISBN 0-89587-247-1 (alk. paper)
1. Kentucky—Guidebooks. 2. Couples—Travel—
Kentucky Guidebooks.
I. Sutton, Laura E. II. title.
F449.3.S25 2001
917.6904'44—dc21
00-058062

Contents

To my family, especially to the memory of my grandparents.—LWS

To three generations of Kentucky couples: my grandparents Raymond and Elizabeth Sutton and Mason and Lora Moore; parents Ray and Sandie Sutton; and brother and sister-in-law Chip and Rebecca Sutton, newlywed Kentuckians who are temporarily finding romance in Kansas.—LES

Acknowledgments

We are indebted to fellow Kentuckians working in chambers of commerce and tourist and visitors bureaus throughout the state. Without their guidance, knowledge, and enthusiasm for their particular corner of the state, this book would be far less interesting or complete. We owe a debt of gratitude to Hill Street Press for conceiving of this project and to Carolyn Sakowski and her terrific staff at John F. Blair, Publisher, for making it a reality. We would like to acknowledge Teresa Collins from the University Press of Kentucky for her expert advice on the state parks; Valerie Smith, formerly of *Kentucky Travel Guide*, and now with *Kentucky Monthly*; and Paul Thomas at the Renfro Valley Visitors Center. We are also indebted to Zoe Ayn Strecker's *Kentucky Off the Beaten Path* for leading us to sites not adequately covered in more traditional state guidebooks. Special thanks to Wade Hall and Kristen Smith for sharing old Kentucky postcards with us.

Finally, Laura would like to acknowledge her friends in Lexington, especially colleagues at the University of Kentucky who were helpful in the writing of this book. Special thanks to Robert E. Rich, who served as enthusiastic guide, chauffeur, dining companion, and all-around romantic partner during the writing of this book.

Leila would like to thank Lisa Dellwo, fellow publicist and author of *Romantic North Carolina* for her advice on how to go about putting this book together. Thanks also go to Mary Jo Dendy for being the best proofreader around.

When one loves somebody, everything is clear—where to go, what to do—it all takes care of itself and one doesn't have to ask anybody about anything.—Maxim Gorki

Introduction Gorki may have had new lovers in mind when he wrote this, because even the most successful romances are occasionally in need of help. Couples young and old know that an occasional jump start is the secret to enduring passion. These jump starts can come in the form of a four-star weekend of dining and lodging; an impromptu hike or quiet wildflower walk; or getting stuck under a covered bridge during a summer rainstorm. It is our hope that this book will provide suggestions for all couples who are looking for promising ways to spend time together, whether it's for an afternoon, evening, weekend getaway, or vacation.

When people think of Kentucky, they often conjure images of thoroughbreds grazing on rolling bluegrass farmland behind miles of white fences, or the strains of "My Old Kentucky Home" on Derby Day. As native Kentuckians, we were both delighted to uncover some of the state's lesser-known charms, particularly those that lend themselves to romance.

Kentucky is blessed with a supreme amount of natural beauty practically everywhere one turns. Nature preserves burst forth with wildflowers in the spring and harbor thriving populations of native birds, butterflies, and mammals. The landscape provides an ideal background for romance, from the unspoiled scenery of Pine Mountain in the east, Kentucky Lake in the west, the Licking River in the north, and Mammoth Cave in south central Kentucky.

In addition, Kentucky boasts one of the finest state park systems in the country. From Jenny Wiley State Resort Park in the mountains of the east to Kentucky Dam Village on the lakes of the west, these parks offer lodging, camping, dining, endless possibilities for recreation, and some of the most breathtaking scenery around. And the state parks certainly keep sweethearts in mind year-round. Many of them offer special weekend getaway packages and host dance or music weekends, photography workshops, or wildlife watches.

In this book, we've taken a broad view of romance and have tried to include something for different lifestyles, interests, and incomes. You'll find everything from a bed and breakfast inn or a riverboat cruise to touring an historic Shaker village or picking blackberries on a scenic farm. Romance is truly wherever one finds it, whether it's the four-star luxuries of a big city, the natural beauty and solitude of a remote mountain village, or the charm and history of a small-town main street.

Finally, we have tried to keep in mind the litmus test posed by a friend who, when trying to prompt her husband to recall their favorite romantic spots in Kentucky, asked, "Come on, honey, where have we taken a bottle of wine together?"

How to Use This Book

Romantic Kentucky is organized thematically, so that suggestions for nature lovers can be found in one chapter, for sports fans in another, for culture vultures in another, and so on. If you're trying to plan an outing in a particular city or locate a specific site, your best bet is to use the index. Some of the special sites in Kentucky are difficult to classify, so we've woven some "Spotlights" between chapters. Furthermore, we want to point out some especially important sites in each chapter, so these are set off in "Highlights." To assist those who live in or who are planning to travel to a particular region, we use geographic codes that accompany each entry. These are:

))))) = **The Golden Triangle: Bluegrass and Northern Kentucky**

⬥ = **Western Waterlands**

▲ = **Eastern Highlands**

〰 =**South Central: Cave and Lake Country**

Romantic Kentucky Hall of Fame

Following are some of our favorite sites and activities in the Bluegrass State sure to kindle the flame:

- ♥ *View the Western hemisphere's only moonbow—a sort of nighttime rainbow—at Cumberland Falls, near Corbin.*
- ♥ *Have breakfast and watch the morning workouts at historic Keeneland Race Track in Lexington.*
- ♥ *Immerse yourself in a weekend of rousing music at the Great American Brass Band Festival in picturesque Danville.*
- ♥ *Enjoy the simple pleasures of an authentic Shaker village.*
- ♥ *Take your sweetheart on the Violet City Lantern Tour at Mammoth Cave.*
- ♥ *Explore some of the one thousand miles of scenic shoreline at Lake Barkley and Kentucky Lake in western Kentucky.*
- ♥ *Take a Moonlight Float on Elkhorn Creek near Frankfort during full-moon weekends.*

♥ Treat yourself to dinner at the four-star Oak Room, followed by an evening at Louisville's famed Seelbach Hotel.

♥ Sleep under the stars in the tranquil mountains at Kingdom Come State Park.

♥ Take a dinner cruise on the Belle of Louisville, the oldest authentic steamboat operating in the country.

HAVE WE LEFT OUT YOUR FAVORITE ROMANTIC THING TO DO IN KENTUCKY?

As we suggested earlier, this book is intended to be an idea book, not an encyclopedic reference. In the appendix, you'll find a listing of further resources to help you research your own outing, including organizations, publications, and websites.

If you'd like the publisher to consider adding your favorite romantic destinations to a future edition, please write:

Romantic Kentucky
John F. Blair, Publisher
1406 Plaza Drive
Winston-Salem, NC 27103
blairpub@blairpub.com

Splendor
in the
Grass

We are lovers of beauty.—Thucydides

We begin the book with a chapter on outdoor wonders partly because Kentucky has so many of them, but also because stars, wildflower trails, and moonlight reflected on a lake just by their very nature inspire romance.

Whether you and your sweetheart love scenic drives, bird-watching, and vineyard tours or like the action found in boating, hiking, or caving, great outdoor dates abound. And as there are countless lakes, rivers, and streams (above and below ground!) throughout the state, you probably will have no trouble finding the perfect place to while away the evening talking and dangling your feet in a cool stream.

BAREFOOT IN THE PARK: GARDENS AND ARBORETUMS

The Book of Life begins with a man and a woman in a garden. It ends with Revelations.—Oscar Wilde

If you love gardens, there's almost nothing more romantic than walking along a winding garden path, spotting a bluebird darting across an open field of wildflowers, or discovering an exotic plant nestled in a wooded glade in a secluded nature preserve. Even the

Department of Transportation is in the spirit, having planted corn poppies, black-eyed Susans, and New England asters along the rights-of-way at various spots throughout the Commonwealth. Whether you prefer formal gardens lined with sweet-smelling boxwood or the unexpected surprises of a rambling hike, a visit to one of Kentucky's parks, gardens, or nature preserves will keep your love in bloom.

The Lexington-Fayette County Arboretum on the campus of the University of Kentucky has come a long way in a few years, just having been named the official state botanical garden. Winding paths in the hundred-acre arboretum are perfect for a jog or a sunset stroll together, and the gazebo at the center of the park provides the focal point for a visit. The area around the building is bursting with collections of annuals and perennials, and nearby benches allow you to sit and enjoy the fragrant breezes. The arboretum also offers an annual stargazing evening in August.

The centerpiece of the arboretum, however, is an absolutely stunning rose garden planted by UK agronomist Tim Phillips. The garden now boasts more than eight hundred roses of all types and colors, with one path featuring the most popular hybrid tea roses from each decade, beginning with the first hybrid tea introduced in 1867. Phillips says that the garden is extremely popular with couples on summer nights with full moons, when the sweet smell of the roses is especially strong.

))))) **University of Kentucky/Lexington - Fayette County Arboretum**
Alumni Drive / Lexington / 859-257-6955

Though small, the Nannie Clay Wallis Arboretum is filled with over seventy varieties of trees (including a number of dogwoods), flowering plants, a rose garden, and a fish pool. The arboretum also houses the headquarters of the Garden Club of Kentucky.

))))) **Nannie Clay Wallis Arboretum**
616 Pleasant Street / Paris / 859-987-6158

Twenty-five miles south of Louisville, Bernheim Forest is a 14,000-acre nature preserve that offers thirty-five miles of marked hiking trails, herb, butterfly, and water gardens, and four lakes. You can while away a summer evening with a fishing pole in hand or visit the nature center and participate in one of the park's outdoor programs. Don't miss the chance to catch a hayride or carriage ride, or sit back and enjoy one of the many outdoor concerts. Guided spring wildflower walks will introduce you to the beauty of bloodroot, trout lily, Virginia bluebells, larkspur, nodding trillium, and shooting star. There's also an unexpected treat; Bernheim is home to an art gallery featuring environmentally themed work by local and regional artists.

))))) **Bernheim Arboretum and Research Forest**
KY 425 / Clermont / 502-955-8512

These two spots won't offer lush vegetation, but they're a bit off the beaten path and they'll get you more in touch with your primordial self. The fossil beds at the Falls of the Ohio date back 400 million years and are one of the world's largest exposed Devonian fossil beds (they were once at the bottom of an inland sea). The Goose Island Fossil Beds, which can be reached by wading across the spillway just below the McAlpine Dam gates at the base of Conrail Bridge, are underwater much of the year. But in the dog days of August when the Ohio River is low, the rocks look something like the surface of the moon. These are magical spots for birders and budding paleontologists, and couples will enjoy finding a quiet haven just a mile away from the hustle and bustle of Louisville.

))) Falls of the Ohio Fossil Beds - Goose Island Fossil Beds
201 West Riverside Drive / Clarksville, IN / 812-280-9970

The Round Table Literary Park is not your typical park, but its unique nature might inspire you to profess your love in verse form. Tucked away in a grove of trees, the park houses replicas of King Arthur's Round Table, the Sword in the Stone, a medieval wall, and a Greco-Roman amphitheater.

Round Table Literary Park
Hopkinsville Community College / Hopkinsville

THE CALL OF THE WILD: NATURE SANCTUARIES

Love is flower-like.—Samuel Taylor Coleridge

Kentucky has eighteen nature preserves, characterized by minimal development in order to protect rare plants and animals. These are ideal spots to get away from it all with your special someone, whether to hike, take pictures, or birdwatch.

Raven Run, with its 374 acres and eight and one half miles of hiking trails, highlights the best of central Kentucky's flora and fauna. Several of the trails at Raven Run offer spectacular views of the Kentucky River Palisades, and the sanctuary sports cascading waterfalls where the three forks of Raven Run converge. There are over three hundred species of wildflowers here, and numerous wildflower walks and a two-day wildflower festival are sponsored here in the spring. In the fall and winter, Raven Run also offers tree identification classes, birdwatching outings, and stargazing evenings. Be sure to look for your bluebird of happiness in the open savannah fields on the trail leading back from the river.

)))) **Raven Run Nature Sanctuary**
Jack's Creek Pike / Lexington / 859-272-6105

If you'd like to go a little wild with your honey, pack a picnic and head for the Salato Center, situated on 132 acres on the west edge of Frankfort. The education center is home to bald eagles, bison, elk, whitetail deer, and turkey. Relax by the edge of a couple of small fishing lakes, explore a wetland, or listen for lovebirds in the songbird area.

)))) **Salato Wildlife Education Center**
I Game Farm Road / Frankfort / 502-564-7863

Though its name sounds naughty, the main attraction at Bad Branch State Nature Preserve is the stunning sixty-foot waterfall that plunges onto boulders below.

▲ **Bad Branch State Nature Preserve**
US-119 on KY-932 / Whitesburg / 502-573-2886

Nearly half of this 554-acre forest is old growth, and these woods are one of Kentucky's only remaining virgin forests. Among the four-hundred-year-old trees, wildflowers abound in the spring.

▲ **Lilley Cornett Woods National Natural Landmark**
KY-1103 West of Whitesburg / 606-633-5828

The Sloughs Wildlife Management Area houses Kentucky's largest blue heron rookery.

Sloughs Wildlife Management Area
KY 268 / Henderson / 270-827-2673

If you are looking for a quiet place to get away from it all, the following wildlife centers and nature preserves will fit the bill.

Jim Beam Nature Preserve
Payne Lane / Nicholasville / 859-259-9655

Clyde E. Buckley Wildlife Sanctuary
1305 Germany Road / Frankfort / 859-873-5711

Logan County Glade State Nature Preserves
US 68 / Russellville / 270-726-2206

Swan Lake Wildlife Management Area
US 60 / Wickliffe / 270-677-2327

West Kentucky Wildlife Management Area
Paducah / 270-488-3233

Woods and Wetlands Wildlife Center
US 68 / Cadiz / 270-522-3892

THE SWEET HEREAFTER: CEMETERIES

When she had passed, it seemed like the ceasing of exquisite music.
—*Henry Wadsworth Longfellow*

A cemetery—romantic? This might seem like an unlikely place for love, but an afternoon stroll around some of the state's beautiful historic cemeteries might just make you more appreciative of your special someone. In her poem "Frankfort Cemetery," Carlisle native Barbara Kingsolver calls it "that kind of place where cars go to be in the dark." Among the memorials and gravestones, you'll discover beautiful testaments of love, giving a small glimpse at some truly great romances of years past.

You could easily spend the better part of a day wandering the three hundred acres of the Cave Hill Cemetery. Its marvelous landscape includes rolling hills, five lakes, and its own cave. There are trees, shrubs, and flowers everywhere you turn, and the graves are clearly lovingly tended. Stop a moment to wonder at the intricate design of a Celtic cross, or rest on a marble bench surrounded by imposing Corinthian columns and a claw-footed fountain. In section thirty-three, you'll find a memorial to Claudia Ellen Sanders, wife of Kentucky Fried Chicken restauranteur Harland Sanders, reminding the world that Claudia was indeed "Truly 'the Colonel's Lady.'"

))))) **Cave Hill Cemetery**
      701 Baxter Avenue / Louisville /
      502-584-8363

Over 150 years old, the Lexington Cemetery has gained a national reputation as an arboretum. The best time to visit is in the spring, when acres of dogwoods and other flowering trees and shrubs are in their full glory. A 120-foot high monument to statesman Henry Clay stands watch over the grounds, and General John Hunt Morgan, the Todd family, and University of Kentucky Coach Adolph

highlight

Louisville Parks

Louisville's three largest parks share the distinction of being designed by noted landscape architect Frederick Law Olmstead, known for his design of New York's Central Park and Atlanta's Piedmont Park. With Cherokee Park in the east, Iroquois in the south, and Shawnee in the west, each park takes advantage of the character and best features of the surrounding neighborhood. With large common areas and graceful walking paths, these parks have given Louisville character and distinction for over one hundred years.

Rupp all found their final resting places in the soothing green spaces of this cemetery. Self-guided tree identification and history walks are available, and over 125 species of birds have been spotted among the vegetation and Victorian sculpture.

))))) **Lexington Cemetery**
833 West Main Street / Lexington / 859-255-5522

The Frankfort Cemetery is one of the loveliest spots in the city. It offers a good view of the domed state capitol as well as a stunning vantage onto the beautiful Kentucky River Palisades, where Daniel Boone's grave stands at the peak of the river overlook. There are some truly wonderful inscriptions to be found among the memorials here. The family of Gabriella Augusta tells the world that she was "warm-hearted, generous, affectionate, and true"—wouldn't we all like to be remembered that way? And the descendants of Catherine Adair, wife of John for fifty-six years, proclaim of the loving couple: "In death they are not divided."

))))) **Frankfort Cemetery**
215 East Main Street / Frankfort / 502-227-2403

OFFBEAT FARMS

If you're looking for a romantic afternoon outing that's off the beaten path, Seldon Scene is a winner. The Llama Trek is a guided hike along some beautiful trails adjacent to the palisades of the Kentucky River; you hike, and the llamas transport a gourmet lunch. Back at the farm, you can check out the llamas, alpacas, and reindeer.

))))) **Seldon Scene Farm**
1710 Watts Ferry Road / Woodford County / 859-873-1622

THE BRIDGES OF FLEMING COUNTY

In their heyday covered bridges were also known as "kissing bridges," places where couples could sneak a kiss as their buggy went through the darkened passage. A reminder of a way of life gone by, covered bridges are wonderful romantic spots for back roads photo ops or for stealing a kiss yourself. There are thirteen covered bridges remaining in Kentucky (the state originally boasted over four hundred), five of which are still open to traffic. Three of the structures are in Fleming County, northeast of Lexington, which calls itself the Covered Bridge Capital of Kentucky (look for the Covered Bridge Festival in August at the Goddard Bridge). Franklin County's Switzer Bridge, which spans the north fork of Elkhorn Creek, has recently been restored after devastating floods.

Call the Kentucky Department of Tourism for directions to the bridges, or check the web site, **www.hultgren.org/things/bridges/ index.htm**, which suggests a two-day tour that will allow you to visit each bridge.

Switzer Bridge (on the North Fork of Elkhorn Creek near Frankfort)

Goddard Bridge (off KY 32, nine miles southeast of Flemingsburg)

Hillsboro Covered Bridge (off KY 411 south of Hillsboro)

Ringo's Mill Bridge (KY 158 near Hillsboro)

Colville Covered Bridge (Route 1893, four miles west of Millersburg)

Johnson Creek Covered Bridge (KY 1029 in Roberston County)

Mt. Zion Covered Bridge (KY 55 near Springfield)

Cabin Creek Covered Bridge (KY 984 in Lewis County)

Dover Covered Bridge (KY 8 at Maysville)

Walcott Covered Bridge (KY 1159 in Bracken County)

Valley Pike Covered Bridge (KY 10 near Maysville)
Oldtown Covered Bridge (KY 1 at Grayson)
Bennett's Mill Bridge (KY 7 at KY 1215 in Greenup County)

THE FRUITS OF YOUR LOVE:
VINEYARDS AND ORCHARDS

Vineyards

No one would mistake Kentucky for the Napa Valley, but wineries and tasting rooms are springing up across the Commonwealth, offering an afternoon outing and a glimpse at what the winemaking process is all about. If you call ahead, the staff at these vineyards will be happy to show you around.

Stop in town for a tasting at Springhill Vineyard's Wine Shop, or check out the vineyard itself in Carrollton, which also hosts concerts and festivals.

 Springhill Vineyard's Wine Shop
125 North Third Street
Bardstown / 502-348-7358

You can pick your own grapes at Barkers in July and August.

 Barkers Blackberry Hill Winery
Crittenden / 859-428-0377

The following three wineries host various special events throughout the year. Take your pick from the Wildflowers and Wine Spring Festival at Broad Run, the

---

highlight

Romantic Placenames

If you're looking for more love on the road, why not get out a map and take a side trip to one of the following charmingly named places in Kentucky:

Beauty
Bliss Blue Moon
Hope
Joy
Lovely
Pinchem Slyly
Pleasureville
Red Hot

Harvest Celebration (complete with live music) at Bravard, or the Big Band and Bacchus celebration at Equus Run.

))))) **Equus Run Vineyards**
1280 Moores Mill Road / Midway / 859-846-9463

))))) **Broad Run Vineyards**
10601 Broad Run Road / Louisville / 502-231-0373

Bravard Vineyards and Winery
15000 Overton Road / Hopkinsville / 270-269-2583

Stop by Chrisman Mill's tasting room to sample their wines, buy Kentucky-made cheese, attend a seminar on wine and food pairings, or take a home winemaking class.

))))) **Chrisman Mill Vineyards**
102 West High Street / Lexington / 859-455-8278

Orchards

We'll take any excuse to get into the great outdoors, but after an afternoon of picking peaches, apples, or blackberries at a local orchard, you have something to show (and eat) for your work. Plus, having your special someone with you means there's someone there to hold the bucket! For a complete listing of roadside farm markets all across the state, contact the Kentucky Farm Bureau at **502-495-5000** or visit their web site at **www.kyfb.com**.

In addition to selling fruits, vegetables, and plants, you can buy homemade bakery goods or enjoy a dish of homemade ice cream topped with fruit.

))))) **Bray's Market House, Orchard and Farm**
       US 42 / Bedford / 502-255-7296

Pick your own pumpkin, or get lost with your sweetheart in the mile-long cornfield maze at It's Fall, You All!

🦃 **It's Fall, You All!**
       7434 Highway 60 East / Henderson / 502-826-8576

Pick your own blackberries, rhubarb, cherries, apples, grapes, and pumpkins at the Berry Farm.

))))) **The Berry Farm**
       Wilsonville Road / Taylorsville / 502-477-2334

Reed's has a wonderful selection of apples, and they even sell "pie bags"—a variety of different apples that are just the right mix of flavors and textures for a fabulous apple pie. (Nothing says love like homemade pie, right?) After picking your produce, you can spread out a blanket and picnic along an old stagecoach trail where Frank and Jesse James once camped.

))))) **Reed's Apple Valley**
       290 Lail Lane / Paris / 859-987-6480

Pick your own apples, or pick up some wonderful fruit the easy way in Garrett's market (make sure to try their caramel-covered apples). The scenic drive is worth the trip.

))))) **Garrett's Orchard & Country Market**
       3360 Highway 1967 South / Lexington / 859-873-3819

Though its name might not inspire romance, the Double Stink Hog Farm's seasonal events offer plenty of fun. Pick your own pumpkin or take a hayride with your honey.

))))) **Double Stink Hog Farm**
5312 Paris Road / Georgetown / 502-863-3437

Don't miss Reid's Orchard Apple Festival in October. During the summer and fall, Reid's lets you pick your own produce.

◣ **Reid's Orchard**
KY 144 / Owensboro / 270-685-2444

MAKING WAVES: LOVE ON THE WATER

Riverboats

You just can't beat a riverboat for romance—moonlight, the wind in your hair, and a special someone by your side. Many of the boats listed below offer dinner cruises.

For over eighty-five years, countless couples have met, had their first dates, or even been married aboard the *Belle*—she's quite the matchmaker! One former passenger remembers: "I was sixteen years old the summer of 1951. What a summer to remember with radiant nights on the boat. To a young girl, those nights were magic—standing on the deck with my current crush, feeling the cool breeze and looking at the stars was romance in the first degree." Watch the sun dip below the horizon on a sunset cruise or heat things up with the Saturday Night Party Cruise on the oldest authentic steamboat operating in the U.S.

))))) *The Belle of Louisville / Spirit of Jefferson*
401 West River Road / Louisville / 502-574-2992
www.belleoflouisville.org

The *Star of Louisville* offers numerous themed dinner cruises. Try a comedy cruise, one of two Valentine's cruises, or celebrate the King's special day with the Elvis Birthday Cruise! For those of you with a more competitive nature, you can even be part of the Derby Festival activities with the annual steamboat race.

highlight

Abbey of Gethsemani

Located south of Bardstown, the serene Abbey of Gethsemani provides a perfect respite from the hectic pace of day-to-day life. This Order of Cistercian Monks is the largest and oldest in America, and the Trappist monastery is probably now best known as the former home of writer Thomas Merton. Steal an afternoon or an evening away with your beloved, where you can walk along one of the wooded trails or watch the sunset from the top of a hill with nothing but the sound of crickets to disturb you. You can even attend one of the services, and the quiet that characterizes them may give you peace of mind and heart.

**3624 Monks Road,
US 31E to KY-247
Trappist / 502-549-3117**

))))) **Star of Louisville**
151 West River Road / Louisville
502-589-7827

BB Riverboats and the *Dixie Belle* offer cruises affording wonderful views of the Cincinnati skyline. And while you're on the waterfront in Covington, take a walk across the Roebling Suspension Bridge, a prototype of the Brooklyn Bridge, to catch the cool river breezes and admire the city lights.

))))) **BB Riverboats**
One Madison Avenue / Covington
800-261-8500

))))) **Queen City Riverboats**
303 Dodd Drive / Covington
859-292-8687

Departing from Shaker Landing on the banks of the Kentucky, the authentic sternwheel riverboat *Dixie Bell* will take you on a one-hour excursion. Call for a schedule of special cruises spring through fall.

))))) **Dixie Belle Riverboat**
**3501 Lexington Road / Harrodsburg /
859-734-5411**

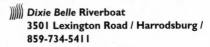

Ferries

If water crossings seem romantic, why not try a trip on a local ferry?

The Valley View Ferry will take you across the Kentucky between Fayette and Madison Counties. Not only is the Valley View unusual since it's an old-fashioned paddlewheel ferry, but it's also one of the oldest businesses in the state—it began operation in 1785.

))))) **Valley View Ferry**
Kentucky River / 859-885-4500

The romantic Augusta Ferry is one of only two working ferries that will transport you across the waters of the Ohio.

))))) **Augusta Ferry**
Ohio River at Augusta / 606-756-3291

A MONTH BY THE LAKE

OK, so you may not have a month to run away and spend time with your sweetheart, but several Kentucky marinas will help you plan a week or weekend getaway that will be just as romantic.

If the clear, cool waters of Laurel Lake are your destination, area marinas have everything you need for a short-term houseboat rental or a waterski weekend. Two of the best are Grove Marina and Holly Bay Marina.

Grove Marina
Corbin / 606-523-2323

Holly Bay Marina
London / 606-864-6542

Located on Lake Barkley, Green Turtle Bay offers plenty of boating and skiing. Or if you'd rather sleep on land, spend the night in one of their condominiums, which come complete with fireplaces and sun porches.

Green Turtle Bay
Grand Rivers / 270-362-8634

THE GREAT OUTDOORS

We love because it's the only true adventure.—Nikki Giovanni

Everywhere you turn in Kentucky, you'll come face to face with natural beauty. Mountains, rivers, streams, and forests will inspire your romantic thoughts and are best shared with someone you love. The state parks are a fabulous resource for heading into the great outdoors, but following are some other areas that you won't want to miss.

Set in the west between Lake Barkley and Kentucky Lake, Land Between the Lakes offers endless possibilities for those romantics who are wild about nature. LBL offers all types of camping, including horse camping, and over seventy miles of horse trails. Hundreds of miles of hiking trails showcase the beauty of woods, fields, and shores, and you can rent a mountain bike or a canoe and set out to observe bald eagles in their natural habitat. A true romantic we know particularly recommends trying a waterside campfire on the pebble beaches that surround Silo Overlook. On a drive through the elk and bison prairie, you can experience how the area looked before pioneer settlement. At the Nature Station, located between Honker and Hermatite Lakes, you can view native endangered species, attend a seminar on wildlife gardening, or take a moonlight canoe ride.

While you're at LBL, save time for a visit to The Homeplace 1850, a working nineteenth-century farm. Enjoy a summer evening of music at one of their pickin' parties or give someone a hint as you watch the recreation of a Homeplace Wedding.

Land Between the Lakes National Recreation Area
100 Van Morgan Drive / Golden Pond / 800-455-5897
www.lbl.org

Grab your honey and head for the Big South Fork, where ninety miles of gorges and valleys abound at this fork of the Cumberland River. In addition to hiking, riding (the area has two horse camps), biking, kayaking, and canoeing, the Big South Fork has special events—such as pioneer encampments and a storytelling festival—throughout the year.

And if you and your mate love to really get away from it all—or need some help in getting away from it all—make a reservation at the **Charit Creek Lodge** (423-429-5704). The lodge can only be reached on foot or horseback, and it has no phones or electricity.

Big South Fork National Recreation Area
4564 Leatherwood Road
Oneida, TN
423-569-9778 or 931-879-3625
www.nps.gov/biso

highlight

The Zoo: Louisville

A trip to the zoo is something like a year-round safari. Heat things up with a stroll through the zoo's steamy rain forest, while crocodiles swim at your feet and birds soar overhead. Let the woolly monkeys make you laugh, or you can admire—but keep your distance from—Siberian tigers, maned wolves, and golden lion tamarinds. The zoo houses over thirteen hundred animals in natural settings; if you're feeling really adventurous, see if you can convince your sweetheart to take a ride on a camel or an elephant.

1100 Trevilian Way
Louisville / 502-459-2181

Red River Gorge lies in the Daniel Boone National Forest in eastern Kentucky, where more than one hundred natural stone arches grace the area. If you're looking for some time for just the two of you, the Clifty Wilderness—over 12,000 acres designated as undeveloped wilderness—offers cliffs, rock shelters, and stream valleys for you to explore. The arch known as Sky Bridge provides an expansive view over the Clifty Wilderness.

If you'd like to check into rock climbing here, get in touch with the **Red River Gorge Climbers' Coalition** at **859-335-0067**. For guided rock climbing, rappelling, caving, canoeing, and backpacking (as well as supplies), contact **Natural Heights (888-737-9036)**.

))))) **Red River Gorge Geological Area**
  Stanton / 606-663-2852

highlight

Rock Fences

The rock fences made of native limestone are the highlights of several of the central Kentucky scenic driving tours. These distinctive walls and fences—often made without mortar—were built before the Civil War by immigrant stonemasons from Ireland assisted by slaves who quarried the rock and later learned the mason's art themselves. For some of the best examples of rock fences, take a leisurely trip along the Paris Pike, Old Frankfort Pike, Pisgah Pike, or the Midway-Versailles Road, all in central Kentucky.

THE SHELTERING SKY: CAMPING

Sleeping under a canopy of trees in a light, airy tent is a joy like no other.—Walt Whitman

There are a number of places to pitch your tent with your sweetheart in Kentucky, especially at the state parks, but these non-park sites come highly recommended.

Located on the west side of Cave Run Lake, Zilpo is a 355-acre site that offers modern amenities and spectacular natural views. The area around Cave Run is home to turkey, deer, fox, bobcats, Canadian geese, bald eagles, and the common loon (and no, that's not your mate). Take in the landscape at the Tater Knob Lookout Tower or frolic at the beach before settling into your campsite for the evening.

Zilpo Recreation Area
Zilpo / 877-444-6777

Bandy Creek is set at the edge of the Big South Fork Recreation Area, minutes from a breathtaking gorge overlook onto the Devil's Jump rapids. From here, you're just a short distance from Yahoo Falls, a 113-foot waterfall surrounded by woodlands (take KY 700 north from Bandy Creek).

Bandy Creek Campground
Stearns / 931-879-4869

TUNNELS OF LOVE: CAVES

Love which in spite of darkness brought us hither,
Should in despite of light keep us together.—John Donne

You'll find the longest system of caverns and cave passages in the world right under your feet in south central Kentucky. You and your sweetheart can gaze at the unique rock formations and other strange, glittering wonders of nature.

With over 350 miles of explored caves and more than fifteen different tours to choose from, there's a lot to see at this World Heritage Site. Try the Violet City Lantern Tour during which, by the light of a coal-oil lantern, you'll learn about the cave's unusual history as a saltpeter mine and a hospital, or take the Gothic Lantern Tour—again by lantern light—to recreate how early explorers experienced the caves. The tours are crowded during peak seasons, so make sure to call ahead for reservations.

If small spaces make you nervous, there's also plenty to keep lovers occupied above ground. Spend the day canoeing along the Green and Nolin Rivers or explore some of the seventy miles of marked nature trails.

Mammoth Cave National Park
Mammoth Cave / 270-758-2328

The Horse Cave area abounds with underground rivers, and Hidden River will book you on an eco-tour on which you and your sweetheart can explore undeveloped portions of the cave and perhaps even glimpse a rare blind cavefish.

Hidden River Cave
119 East Main Street / Horse Cave
270-786-1466

See the largest cave opening east of the Mississippi as well as the shortest, deepest river in the world at the Lost River Cave Valley. In past decades, the cave doubled as an underground nightclub. Today, Lost River boasts a nature trail, as well as a butterfly house and gardens designed to attract native Kentucky butterflies.

Lost River Cave Valley
US 31 and Cave Mill Road
Bowling Green
270-793-1023

Billing itself as the Gem of America's Caves, Diamond Caverns is a privately owned cave located just outside Mammoth Cave National Park. Marvel at over one thousand stalactites, stalagmites, and flowstone, with names like Victoria Falls and Angel's Veil. If you're really looking for an unusual place to tie the knot, say "I do" in the underground Onyx Cathedral.

Diamond Caverns
1878 Mammoth Cave Parkway / Park City
270-749-2223

spotlight

TWO FOR THE ROAD
Driving Tours

Two people shorten a road.—Irish Proverb

Sometimes, what a good romance needs is a little change of scenery. Find a warm afternoon, roll down the windows, turn up the radio, and hit the road. From the Purchase area in the west to the mountains in the east, Kentucky has twelve drives classified as scenic byways that are sure to get the heart going. Call the Kentucky Department of Travel (800-225-TRIP) for a driving map.

Begin with a view of the majestic Mississippi from Columbus-Belmont State Park, then stop at the Fulton County Courthouse to see the oldest non-electric clock in Kentucky. Wind up your journey at Reelfoot National Wildlife Refuge at the Tennessee state line.

))))) Great River Road

Start with a bite to eat around the former home of writer and food expert Duncan Hines near Bowling Green. Meander through several historic communities, spend a little time in the dark at Mammoth Cave, and cross the Green River by ferry.

⚓ Duncan Hines Tour

The scenic and historic Cordell Hull Highway connects Mammoth Cave in Kentucky to the Great Smoky Mountains in

Tennessee. Visit the Old Mulkey Meeting House, the first church west of the Appalachians, or take time to smell the flowers at the Heritage Gardens. Also called the Rollercoaster Highway, the Cordell Hull drive winds through the hills and valleys of rural Kentucky.

Cordell Hull Highway

Originally an animal trace, the Old Kentucky Turnpike was the main route from the Falls of the Ohio to Nashville. Stop in Bardstown to experience the romance of the *Stephen Foster Story*, an outdoor drama, or savor the scenery of the Rolling Fork River Valley.

spotlight

TWO FOR THE ROAD
Driving Tours

Old Kentucky Turnpike

This seven-mile drive in Louisville borders the Ohio River. Begin your trip at the Six-Mile Island Nature Preserve and finish at the Louisville Water Company 1860 Water Tower, a national Historic Landmark that is also the location of the Louisville Art Association.

River Road

Cruise along US 68 to see one of the longest continuous stretches of rock fences in Kentucky. The drive passes through the peaceful and scenic Shaker Village outside Harrodsburg and alongside the Kentucky River where the *Dixie Belle* riverboat is moored.

Shakertown

The drive along Old Frankfort and Pisgah Pikes is the stuff of Kentucky postcards. Rock fences, horse farms, and green rolling hills characterize this trip through the heart of the bluegrass. See old Kentucky homes and churches while traveling through one of the largest rural historic districts in Kentucky.

))))) Old Frankfort and Pisgah Pikes

Start a wonderful daytrip at the Boone County Cliffs, enjoy the scenery at the Dinsmore Woods State Nature Preserve, then travel back in time at the Big Bone Lick State Park, one of the country's major archaeological sites.

))))) Big Bone Lick State Park

The drive along Riverboat Row highlights the sights and sounds of life along the Ohio River. Dine on a floating restaurant on the river, then go for an after-dinner stroll at James Taylor Park. The Historic Riverwalk allows for a breathtaking view of the Cincinnati skyline, with the city lights reflected in the water.

))))) Riverboat Row

Beginning in Fayette County near Athens, the drive along Boone Creek winds past palisades, waterfalls, and lush vegetation. Along the way you'll see the Grimes Mill Historic Complex, home of the Iroquois Hunt Club and a water-powered gristmill made of local limestone and dating from 1805.

))))) Boone Creek

---

highlight

Pisgah Presbyterian Church

Established in 1784, Pisgah Presbyterian Church was the first Presbyterian church west of the Allegheny Mountains. The building dates to 1812, with pioneers and Revolutionary War veterans buried in the adjacent cemetery. Set among the shady trees and rolling hills of a Kentucky Scenic Byway, this tiny chapel with old stained glass windows makes a great romantic stop, whether you're planning a wedding or just out for a drive.

Pisgah Pike
Lexington / 859-873-4161

spotlight

TWO FOR THE ROAD
Driving Tours

A trek along US 68 highlights some of the state's rich heritage. The tour starts at the Blue Licks Battlefield, the site of Kentucky's last battle of the Revolutionary War. Head north to Maysville, a picturesque river city where you can catch a ferry or a riverboat for an afternoon outing.

)))) US 68

An eight-mile jaunt will take you up Pine Mountain, from which you can marvel at the Appalachian Mountains and the Jefferson National Forest. Trails leading off the mountain showcase a variety of wildflowers and rock formations.

Pine Mountain

Heart-
stopping
Locales:
State
Parks

I will make you brooches and toys for your delight
Of birdsong at morning and starshine at night.—Robert Louis Stevenson

If it's true that love blooms in the presence of beauty, natives of and visitors to Kentucky couldn't ask for a finer state for romance. Natural beauty abounds in all parts of the state, from the majestic mountains of the east to the green, rolling hills of central Kentucky to the cool, deep lakes of the west. And there is perhaps no better way to enjoy the breathtaking variety of the Commonwealth's natural wonders than a visit to one of Kentucky's state parks.

Often touted as the nation's finest, the state park system has just what lovers need for a special weekend trip, or even just a day captured from the hectic pace of everyday life. Hiking, boating, horseback riding, birdwatching, swimming, camping—the parks pretty much have it all.

The park system in Kentucky is divided into three categories. The Kentucky Resort Parks contain everything you need for an extended stay, including overnight lodging (in most parks, this involves both lodges and cabins) and dining facilities; most of these parks also have golf courses and are situated by lakes. Recreational Parks feature camping and a host of outdoor activities. State Historic Sites are parks featuring places or buildings of importance in Kentucky's history.

Many of the parks offer special activities (ranging from story-telling to craft festivals to photography workshops) throughout the year, so be sure to call for a schedule (**800-255-PARK**) or check the state park web site at **www. kystateparks.com**. Even the state park system encourages your romance—ask about special Sweetheart Weekend packages at the resort parks, which include lodging and meals. Remember that at the parks, dinner hours are early, and many counties are dry.

EASTERN HIGHLANDS

Jenny Wiley State Resort Park is located in the heart of the Appalachian Mountains at the side of the eleven-hundred-acre Dewey Lake. The park has a lodge and eighteen cabins and features ten miles of scenic hiking trails and a mountain bike trail. Don't miss the skylift that will take you to the top of Sugar Camp Mountain where, on a clear day, you and your special someone can enjoy a view of sixty surrounding miles. The Jenny Wiley Theatre is another great romantic feature of the park where you can enjoy musical theater under the stars.

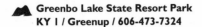 **Jenny Wiley State Resort Park**
39 Jenny Wiley Road / Prestonsburg / 606-886-2711

Author, educator, and state poet laureate Jesse Stuart holds a special place at Greenbo Lake State Resort Park. The fieldstone lodge is named in his honor, and in a special reading room you can get acquainted with one of Kentucky's most beloved writers. Hikers will be in heaven here—you and your sweetheart can explore twenty-five miles of trails in over three thousand acres of pristine forest.

Greenbo Lake State Resort Park
KY 1 / Greenup / 606-473-7324

The main attraction at Grayson Lake State Park is the lake—fifteen hundred acres of it surrounded by tall sandstone bluffs. Two long, linked trails showcase flowering rhododendron and pass alongside Lick Falls. On summer weekends, the park also features the outdoor drama *Someday,* a story of love and war set in eastern Kentucky in the 1860s.

▲▲ **Grayson Lake State Park**
   314 Grayson Lake Park Road / Olive Hill / 606-474-9727

For those romantics who like a little adventure, Carter Caves is for you. Head underground for a lighted (or unlighted!) cave tour, and don't miss Cascade Cave, noted for its beauty and for a thirty-foot underground waterfall. Take a boat out on Smokey Valley Lake, canoe down Tygart's Creek, or take a trail ride through the forested hills before heading back to the stone lodge or a private cabin.

▲▲ **Carter Caves State Resort Park**
   344 Caveland Drive / Olive Hill / 606-286-4411

Set deep in the mountains, this lake is one of the state's undiscovered treasures. The lake is surrounded by steep cliffs and shady coves, making it the perfect spot for a houseboating weekend.

▲▲ **Paintsville Lake State Park**
   KY 40 / Paintsville / 606-297-5253

Set at the crest of Pine Mountain, this park has an extraordinary view—from 2,700 feet—of more than a thousand acres of unspoiled wilderness. One Kentuckian we know says that Kingdom Come is "nature the way God intended." Hiking trails include rugged scenery and plenty of overlooks. Unusual rock formations abound, such as Log Rock, a natural sandstone bridge, or Raven Rock, a rock exposure reaching 290 feet into the sky.

Kingdom Come State Park
US 119 / Cumberland / 606-589-2479

Located in the hills surrounding the edge of the Daniel Boone National Forest, Buckhorn features a twelve-hundred-acre lake, beach, pool, hiking trails, and miniature golf. The main lodge has a large veranda with great views in addition to a copper-hooded fireplace for cooler nights. Look for special weekend events throughout the year, including the Mountain Showcase and Bird Watch/Wildflower Walk in the spring and the Elk Watch weekend in the fall.

Buckhorn Lake State Resort Park
4441 Kentucky Highway 1833 / Buckhorn / 606-398-7510

Follow the path of Kentucky pioneers in one of the early areas of settlement in the state. Levi Jackson Wilderness Road State Park has over eight miles of hiking trails on the Wilderness Road and Boone's Trace, and the Mountain Life Museum and McHargue's Mill will let you glimpse what life was like in another century along the shaded banks of the Laurel River.

Levi Jackson Wilderness Road State Park
998 Levi Jackson Mill Road / London / 606-878-8000

Some of the most beautiful mountain scenery in Kentucky will stop your heart in Kentucky's first state park, Pine Mountain State Resort Park. In addition to the lodge and cottages, log cabins at the park feature private decks and stone fireplaces. Over eight miles of hiking trails include a trail to Chained Rock, which offers spectacular views of Pineville, the route of the Wilderness Road, and the Cumberland Mountain Ridge. Pine Mountain is also the site of the annual Mountain Laurel Festival, a celebration including dances, concerts, and fireworks held each May in a forest cove that has been transformed into an amphitheater. For a weekend getaway when you feel like trying something new, the park offers special programs such as the New Astronomers Weekend in the spring or a fall photography workshop weekend.

An added attraction is the nearby **Cumberland Gap National Historical Park** in Middlesboro (**606-248-2817**). Cumberland Gap was the natural pass that settlers traveled to cut through the Allegheny Mountains. Visit Pinnacle Overlook for a breathtaking panoramic view of three states.

▲▲ **Pine Mountain State Resort Park**
     1050 State Park Road / Pineville / 606-337-3066

Camping and water sports are at the heart of a trip to 2,300-acre Yatesville Lake. Once you've explored the lake's three islands, the park serves as a good home base for a visit to nearby US 23, also known as The Country Music Highway. The highway marks the birthplaces of Kentucky's twelve top country music stars.

▲▲ **Yatesville Lake State Park**
     KY 3215 / Louisa / 606-673-1490

Nestled in the Daniel Boone National Forest, Natural Bridge is a favorite romantic spot for daytrippers who want to get out of the house to explore the beauty of the changing seasons. The jewel of the park is a seventy-eight-foot-long by sixty-five-foot-high natural sandstone arch. Make a point to stay longer in Hemlock Lodge or in a cottage, take a ride on the skylift, or visit **Hoedown Island (606-669-6650)**, an open-air dance patio by the lake that features weekly square dances.

▲▲ **Natural Bridge State Resort Park**
     2135 Natural Bridge Road / Slade / 859-663-2214

Sitting on the Kentucky/Virginia border, the Breaks is highly rec-ommended for stunning scenery. From hiking trails and scenic overlooks, you can marvel at the largest canyon east of the Mississippi. The Russell Fork River winds over five miles through sixteen-hundred-foot cliffs, which explains why some have called this area the Grand Canyon of the South. Don't miss rafting on the class VI rapids!

Breaks Interstate Park
KY/VA 80 / Breaks, VA / 540-865-4413

THE GOLDEN TRIANGLE:
BLUEGRASS AND NORTHERN KENTUCKY

An abundance of outdoor activities make Kincaid Lake a good choice for those who love to camp. Spend the day on the 183-acre lake—rent a pontoon boat or pedal boat, or row your way past miles of scenic shoreline.

Kincaid Lake State Park
KY 159 / Falmouth / 859-654-3531

First the site of salt springs that attracted animals and pioneers to the area, Blue Licks became better known as the site of the last Revolutionary War battle in Kentucky. Also the spot where Daniel Boone was kidnapped by Native Americans, Blue Licks has a newly built lodge to serve as the center of your trip back in time.

Blue Licks Battlefield State Resort Park
US 68 / Mount Olivet / 800-443-7008

Big Bone Lick is a tribute to the prehistory of the region. Fifteen thousand years ago, giant mammoths, mastodons, and bison roamed these swamplands and visited the salt licks. Though fishing, camping, and hiking are the order of the day today, a discovery trail features a glimpse of what early life here was like. The park even has its very own buffalo herd.

))))) **Big Bone Lick State Park**
3380 Beaver Road / Union / 859-384-3522

White Hall was the home of Cassius Marcellus Clay, abolitionist and politician (now perhaps best remembered for taking a child bride in his late years). The Italianate mansion has now been restored to its 1860s splendor; don't miss a special tour, A Haunted Evening with the Clay Family, which will—literally—bring you closer to your honey lest either of you be carried off by a wayward spirit. During the holiday season, White Hall also offers candlelight tours (and who doesn't look good by candlelight?).

))))) **White Hall State Historic Site**
500 White Hall Shrine Road / Richmond / 859-623-9178

With a scenic overlook set at the confluence of the Kentucky and Ohio Rivers, General Butler State Resort Park honors two Kentucky military families. Tour the Butler-Turpin home, built in 1859, or spend the night at the hilltop lodge. Make sure to go for the annual Kentucky Scottish Weekend in May, which celebrates highland music, dance, and sport.

))))) **General Butler State Resort Park**
US 42 / Carrollton / 502-732-4384

Set at the outskirts of the Louisville metropolitan area, E. P. "Tom" Sawyer State Park offers a wide array of indoor and outdoor activities. Cool off in the Olympic-size pool, jog the one-mile fitness trail, or take a leisurely walk along the Goose Creek nature trail. Watch for special events throughout the year, including the outdoor Corn Island Storytelling Festival in September.

))))) **E. P. "Tom" Sawyer State Park**
   3000 Freys Hill Road / Louisville / 502-426-8950

Spend the night under the stars in Taylorsville Lake State Park campground or cozy up to your mate at one of the horse campsites. The park offers seventeen miles of wooded horse trails and great fishing on the three-thousand-acre lake.

))))) **Taylorsville Lake State Park**
   KY 248 / Taylorsville / 502-477-8766

Also known as Federal Hill, My Old Kentucky Home honors the house that supposedly inspired Stephen Foster's song of the same name. The home has been lovingly restored to its antebellum glory, and Christmas Candlelight tours (which recreate an elaborate 1800s holiday) should put you in the sprit of the season. This area is also home to *The Stephen Foster Story*, an outdoor musical featuring over fifty of Foster's beloved songs (**800-626-1563** for reservations).

))))) **My Old Kentucky Home State Park**
   US 150 / Bardstown / 800-323-7803

Abraham Lincoln's mother settled in this plain near the Beech Fork River, and you can still visit her original cabin, as well as other period replicas. And if you and your partner are both into golf, you can spend the afternoon playing eighteen holes amid the green, rolling hills.

))))) **Lincoln Homestead State Park**
   5079 Lincoln Park Road / Springfield / 606-336-7461

A visit to Old Fort Harrod is a great outing for those lovers who love history. During the spring and summer months, the site of the first permanent settlement west of the Alleghenies becomes a living history experience where costumed guides recreate pioneer life. You can even visit the cabin where Abraham Lincoln's parents were married in 1806.

))))) **Old Fort Harrod State Park**
US 68 / Harrodsburg / 859-734-3314

As interest in the Civil War booms, explore the site of Kentucky's most devastating battle of the war at Perryville Battlefield State Historic Site. Each October, reenactors commemorate the South's last major campaign to capture the state.

))))) **Perryville Battlefield State Historic Site**
1825 Battlefield Road / Perryville / 859-332-8631

What began as a pioneer outpost, later became an important trade center and still later a mineral spring resort, has now been reconstructed as a working fort along the banks of the Kentucky River. Check out the pioneer craft demonstrations of the self-guided river walk trail, which showcases the flora, fauna, and geographical and historic sites along the river's edge.

))))) **Fort Boonesborough State Park**
4375 Boonesborough Road / Richmond / 859-527-3131

Take some time just for the two of you in Rough River Dam State Resort Park's secluded lodge overlooking a 5,000-acre lake. Rough River will get your toes tapping in July during the annual Official Kentucky State Championship Old Time Fiddler's Contest.

))))) **Rough River Dam State Resort Park**
450 Lodge Road / Falls of Rough / 800-325-1713

Featuring a spectacular waterfall known as the Niagra of the South, Cumberland Falls State Resort Park rates as one of the state's top romantic spots. The 125-foot wide falls drop sixty feet, and moonlight passing through the resulting heavy mist creates the only moonbow—a sort of nighttime rainbow—in the Western hemisphere. (The moonbow is visible only on clear nights with a full moon, so make sure to call the park for optimum viewing dates.) The main lodge at the park features a large stone fireplace, and most of the cottages have their own fireplace. Hikers will delight in over seventeen miles of lush trails, including the Moonbow Trail. Take a guided trail ride or try an exciting white-water rafting trip among the park's rapids.

))))) **Cumberland Falls State Resort Park**
   7351 Highway 90 / Corbin / 606-528-4121

SOUTH CENTRAL: CAVE AND LAKE COUNTRY

A fabulous spot for pleasure boating spanning over fifty thousand acres, Lake Cumberland has houseboats, pontoons, and ski boats available. Choose from either of two lodges, or reserve a cozy cottage complete with fireplace. You can also hike or take a guided trail ride along the lake.

Lake Cumberland State Resort Park
   5465 State Park Road / Jamestown / 270-343-3111

General Burnside is Kentucky's only island state park and features camping and golf. The park is also worth a visit during the holiday season, when Christmas Island's special light displays help put visitors in the mood of the season.

General Burnside State Park
   US 27 / Burnside / 606-561-4104

The new limestone and timber lodge at Dale Hollow looks down on a serene 2,800-acre lake. There are plenty of secluded inlets and small islands dotting the lake, so it will be easy to feel like you're the only two people around for miles. The park also offers twenty-four horse camping sites along forested riding trails.

Dale Hollow Lake State Resort Park
6371 State Park Road / Bow / 270-433-7431

Settle in among the forested hills, where you can camp, spend the night in a lodge overlooking the lake, or overnight in a cottage. Spend the day fishing, boating, swimming, hiking, or horseback riding at Barren River Lake, or drive to the nearby Mammoth Cave National Park. Barren River is the site of the Glasgow Highland Games in June and a Halloween Spookout in October.

Barren River Lake State Resort Park
1149 State Park Road / Lucas / 270-646-2151

Over 8,200 acres of water await you at Green River. Rent a houseboat or ski boat, or cool off in the beach area. Play a little on the twenty-mile hiking and mountain bike trails, or challenge your sweetheart to a round of miniature golf at the campground.

Green River Lake State Park
179 Park Office Road / Campbellsville / 270-465-8255

Bordered by Pennyrile Forest and Lake Beshear, the park offers a great spot for canoeing. Commune with nature—and each other—on one of the hiking trails among the park's 863 acres. From July through September, make sure to look for the pennyroyal (also called pennyrile), a small violet flower from whence the area forest takes its name. Pennyrile has a new Olympic-sized swimming pool and both a lodge and lakeside or woodland cottages with porches or fireplaces (cottage #508 is a favorite). The park hosts an annual Sweetheart Weekend, which includes accomodations and special activities in the romantic stone lodge, as well as offering a photography weekend and a country-western weekend.

Pennyrile Forest State Resort Park
20781 Pennyrile Lodge Road / Dawson Springs / 800-325-1711

WESTERN WATERLANDS

Nature lovers will enjoy this getaway just south of the Ohio River. John James Audubon, who lived in Henderson for several years, was the first artist to draw life-sized birds and animals in their natural habitats. Marvel at the collection of Audubon's watercolors and oil paintings, then step outside and see the birds for yourself! Over six miles of hiking and backcountry trails give you the chance to spot over 170 species of birds. Five one-bedroom cottages lie nestled in the woods here. The park also plays host to the Big River Arts and Crafts Festival in October, the state's second largest craft fair.

John James Audubon State Park
US 60 / Henderson / 270-826-2247

The secluded three-hundred-acre lake at Lake Malone State Park has impressive rock bluffs. Primitive camping is a delight here, where you and your sweetheart can wander among the mountain laurel, dogwoods, and hollies before settling in at night to enjoy the starlight and the gentle music of cicadas.

Lake Malone State Park
KY 973 / Dunmore / 270-657-2111

From the vantage of the wonderful half-circle-shaped lodge, thrill at the vast expanse of Lake Barkley. With over one thousand miles of shoreline, Barkley and adjoining Kentucky Lake create the largest man-made body of water in the world.

Lake Barkley State Resort Park
US 68 / Cadiz / 800-325-1708

One of the most popular resort parks in the state, Kentucky Dam Village sits between Lake Barkley and Kentucky Lake. Water sports are the best at this massive 160,000-acre body of water, and you can rent a pontoon boat for a lazy day of sunning and swimming or chase your loved one around on a wave runner! A lovely feature of this park is nearby Land Between the Lakes, a lush, forty-mile long nature conservation area. And if all this isn't enough to fire up your sense of romance, to celebrate Valentine's Day, the park hosts an old-fashioned Country Sweetheart Weekend, a package which includes lodging, entertainment, country-western dance lessons, and culminates with a dinner dance.

Kentucky Dam Village State Resort Park
US 641 / Gilbertsville / 270-362-4271

On the middle western shore of Kentucky Lake, Kenlake offers the best site for big boat sailing in the state. It also features an indoor tennis center and the Twilight Cabaret, as well as a week-end designed to let you get to know eagles in their habitat. And as everyone knows, you can't really beat the summer heat in Kentucky, so you might as well revel in it at the Hot August Blues Festival held at Kenlake.

Kenlake State Resort Park
542 Kenlake Road / Hardin / 800-325-0143

The area around what is today the Columbus-Belmont Battlefield State Park was of vital importance to Union forces during the Civil War and marked General Ulysses S. Grant's first active engagement as he tried to capture a stronghold on the Mississippi River. Today, lovers can muse on the strife of yesteryear (the hiking trails run alongside bluffs and earthenworks that made up Confederate trenches) but enjoy a much more peaceful stay at a campground overlooking the mighty Mississippi.

 Columbus-Belmont Battlefield State Park
KY 123/80 / Columbus / 270-677-2327

spotlight

FAIRS AND FESTIVALS

Kentuckians love to celebrate their handicrafts, their folk-ways, and the special things that make their particular part of the state unique. In previous chapters we've listed some of these annual events in conjunction with other activities or places, but there are more celebrations we don't want to leave out. We don't pretend that this gathering is comprehensive—there are hundreds of festivals stretching to every corner of the state—but the following is a good start for lovers wanting to experience the variety of Kentucky folk life.

Stretching over eleven days in August, the Kentucky State Fair is an ideal place for sweethearts of any age. Ride the ferris wheel, win your date a stuffed animal, savor Kentucky barbecue, marvel at the state's biggest pumpkin, and enjoy the fun of livestock competitions.

))))) **Kentucky State Fair**
Kentucky Fair and Exposition Center / Louisville
502-367-5180

One of the biggest celebrations in the state, the three-week Kentucky Derby Festival is a fitting buildup to the greatest two minutes in sport. Beginning with Thunder Over Louisville, a military air-show and spectacular fireworks display, the festival continues with the Pegasus Parade, the Great Steamboat Race, and concerts. The highlight is the "balloon glow" in which all of the balloons in town for the race put on quite a show; at dusk they fire up and look like dozens of colorful jewels against the night sky.

 **Kentucky Derby Festival**
Louisville / 800-928-FEST

FAIRS AND FESTIVALS

Celebrate spring or welcome the harvest in a German-inspired village near the Ohio River at Maifest and Oktoberfest. Music, food, crafts, and rides let you experience a little of the German vacation you may have missed. And if you can't make it to New Orleans this year either, don't worry. MainStrasse puts on a Mardi Gras celebration complete with floats, bands, and Cajun entertainment.

 **Maifest and Oktoberfest**
MainStrasse Village / Covington / 513-357-MAIN

The American Quilter's Society National Quilt Show is a tribute to a beautiful traditional art form. Hundreds of quilts from all over the world go on display, and the show has been named one of the top hundred events in North America by a popular tour organizer.

 **American Quilter's Society National Quilt Show**
Paducah / 270-898-3757

The W. C. Handy Blues and Barbecue Festival is Henderson's tribute to its own renowned blues musician and composer. Good music and fantastic barbecue make for a date that's hard to beat.

 **W. C. Handy Blues and Barbecue Festival**
Henderson / 800-648-3128

An impressive array of artists and craftspeople are drawn to the St. James Court Art Show each October. And why not? The St. James Court neighborhood in Louisville has got to be one of the most romantic in the state, with its large shade trees and ornately designed and lovingly tended Victorian-, Gothic-, Italianate-, and Beaux Arts-style homes.

))))) **St. James Court Art Show**
Central Park / Louisville / 502-635-5244

The Kentucky Folklife Festival is a joint venture by the Kentucky Historical Society and the Kentucky Arts Commission to celebrate the state's various folk and ethnic traditions. You and your date can enjoy performances; craft demonstrations such as wood carving or chairmaking; and—what would any fair be without it?—food.

))))) **Kentucky Folklife Festival**
Frankfort / 502-564-1792

Can't
Give you
Anything
But Love

Love has nothing to do with what you are expecting to get—only with what you are expecting to give—which is everything.—Katharine Hepburn

Kentucky is crafts, antiques, and folk art country. Many communities large and small feature shopping districts with rows of antique stores or shops featuring locally made art, pottery, rugs, baskets, and just about anything else you can imagine. Berea, with its many artist studios and crafts stores, and Bybee Pottery in Waco are two of the most popular shopping destinations in the state, if not the region.

ANTIQUES

Shopping for antiques combines the fun of aimless browsing with the thrill of unexpected discovery. Come to think of it, antique shopping may be a perfect analogy for romance, which is why we recommend it as an activity for couples who are looking for ways to spend time together. After all, both require lots of time hunting before you find that perfect something (or someone) with which you want to spend the rest of your life. And what better way for two people to reveal themselves to each other than by rediscovering the Mrs. Beasley doll she slept with until she was ten, or the carved walnut sideboard that reminds him of Thanksgiving at his grandmother's house?

Below we have given a sampling of the state's antiques outlets, recommending that you plan to visit towns or regions that offer a cluster of stores. Georgetown in central Kentucky boasts the state's largest collection of antique dealers and is known as the state's Antiques Capital. Tiny Hazel on the Tennessee border is western Kentucky's oldest and largest antique shopping district with more than twelve shops and malls.

Antique stores are notorious for closing (or opening!) overnight, so contact the relevant chamber of commerce or tourist bureau before you set off on a day of antiquing in Kentucky.

An incomplete list of towns we recommend for exploring includes Franklin; Augusta; Elizabethtown; Glendale; Versailles; Harrodsburg; Hopkinsville; Columbia (also offers locally made crafts and furniture); Bowling Green; Smiths Grove; Springfield; and Danville.

Located near Keeneland and the Bluegrass Airport, Boone's offers one of the largest selections of French, English, and American antiques in the South.

))) **Boone's Antiques of Kentucky, Inc.**
4996 Old Versailles Road / Lexington / 859-254-5335

Look for the knight in shining armor in front of Heritage Antiques. Inside you'll find a wide variety of treasures.

))) **Heritage Antiques**
380 East Main Street / Lexington / 859-253-1035

The Loose Leaf Antiques and Collectibles Show is held once a month, spring through fall. Call ahead for dates for this large and eclectic sale.

))) **Loose Leaf Antique & Collectible Show**
553 Angliana Avenue / Lexington / 859-255-7309

Located in a historic three-story stone house, Head House Antiques and Uniques is surrounded by original outbuildings filled with craft, gift, and antique shops. You may also want to visit The Tiffany Cellar for lunch, tea, or dessert.

))))) **Head House Antiques and Uniques**
The Tiffany Cellar
11601 Main Street / Middletown / 502-245-6695

After shopping at Henry County Heritage House Antiques & Gifts, stop by the **Heritage Tearoom**, which is two doors down.

))))) **Henry County Heritage House Antiques & Gifts**
137 South Main Street / New Castle / 502-845-2422

The drive to the tiny Nonesuch community in rural Woodford County is part of the adventure of visiting Irish Acres. The store displays 32,000 square feet of American and European furniture, glassware, china, crystal, silver, linens, jewelry, rugs, and decorative accessories. Spend the morning shopping, then visit **The Glitz** restaurant for lunch (and more gawking at the over-the-top décor). Open for lunch March through December. We encourage you to phone ahead for reservations (**859-873-6956**).

))))) **Irish Acres Gallery of Antiques**
4205 Ford's Mill Road / Versailles / 859-873-7235

More than three hundred dealers and eighty thousand square feet of antiques are to be found in the eclectic Louisville Antique Mall.

))))) **Louisville Antique Mall and The Café**
900 Goss Avenue / Louisville
502-635-2852 / www.antiqnet.com/louisville

If Hollywood created an antiques store, Joe Ley would be it. Two acres of treasures fill this 1890 schoolhouse. The vast selection, including whimsical and oversized toys, carousel animals, and the occasional clown make this a must-see. Don't miss Mr. Ley's private collection, available to view but not for purchase.

))))) **Joe Ley Antiques, Inc.**
615 East Market Street / Louisville / 502-583-4014

The Historic Danville Antique Mall occupies the upstairs floor of an old Presbyterian church. After you shop, be sure to visit the **Tea Leaf Restaurant and Bookstore** downstairs (enter at 230 West Broadway; 859-236-7456).

))))) **Historic Danville Antique Mall**
158 North Third Street / Danville

ARTS AND CRAFTS

Kentucky handicrafts—traditional, contemporary, and folk art— are collected around the world. More than 4,000 artisans work in the state, and in recognition of this fact, the Kentucky Arts Council launched the Kentucky Craft Marketing Program to promote and develop this industry. For more information about participating artists, contact the Kentucky Craft Marketing Program in Frankfort at **(502) 564-8076**; **www.kycraft.org**.

Hand-blown art glass items are made while you watch and are available for purchase at Hawks View Gallery.

))))) **Hawks View Gallery**
170 Carter Avenue / Louisville / 502-955-1010

At the Kentucky Art and Craft Gallery, located on Louisville's historic Main Street in a restored nineteenth century building, visitors can browse the work of Kentucky artists in two exhibition galleries as well as a gift shop. Most gallery items are available for sale.

))))) **Kentucky Art and Craft Gallery**
609 West Main Street / Louisville
502-589-0102; 800-446-0102

The last Saturday of June, folk art and craft lovers converge on artist Minnie Atkins's Peaceful Valley home for a sale of works by Elliott County artists and craftpersons.

▲ **Folk Art Day in the Country**
Peaceful Valley / 606-738-5779

Located between Berea and Richmond, Bybee Pottery, a Kentucky crafts landmark founded in 1845, is the oldest pottery west of the Alleghenies. The Cornelison family still uses local clay to make its solid-color or speckled trademark wares. You are sure to find a crowd waiting for the doors to open at 8 A. M. on Mondays, Wednesdays, and Fridays, when the gift shop is restocked.

))))) **Bybee Pottery**
610 Waco Loop / Highway 52E / Waco / 859-369-5350

Completely Kentucky carries locally made specialty foods and works by more than 250 of the state's craftspeople.

))))) **Completely Kentucky**
237 West Broadway / Frankfort / 502-223-5240

The museum store at the Kentucky Folk Art Center offers the work of regional contemporary folk artists, along with folk toys, books, and other educational materials.

▲ **Kentucky Folk Art Center**
102 West First Street / Morehead / 606-783-2204

Located five miles west of Cumberland Falls, the Falls Mountain Craft Center sells thousands of items in an 1842 log structure.

Falls Mountain Craft Center
HC 84, Box 283 / Parker's Lake / 606-376-3463

Pine Mountain-Letcher County Crafts Co-Op features works by forty craftspeople as well as demonstrations.

Pine Mountain-Letcher County Crafts Co-Op
US 119 / Whitesburg / 606-663-0185

The Kentucky Haus Craft Gallery is a perfect place to visit before or after an afternoon at the Newport Aquarium, located next door.

Kentucky Haus Craft Gallery
421 Monmouth Street / Newport / 859-261-4287
www.kentuckyhaus.com

Shop the Old Tyme Store for buggies, furniture, baskets, quilts, jellies, and more, all made by the local Amish community.

The Old Tyme Store
Shepherdsville / 502-957-6367

The Jailhouse Arts & Crafts Co-Op is located in a historic jail and houses the work of twenty artists, most of whom are from Spencer County.

Jailhouse Arts & Crafts Co-Op
Courthouse Alley / Taylorsville /502-477-6654

Lexington's Artique is one of the best, most unique shopping experiences in Kentucky. The store's two locations carry the work of hundreds of American artists, with a healthy representation of local work, from fine jewelry to whimsical garden sculptures.

))))) **Artique**
   Lexington Green / Lexington / 859-272-8802

))))) **Artique**
   Civic Center Shops / Lexington / 859-233-1774

GIFT AND SPECIALTY SHOPS

Unique shopping experiences can be found in every region of the state. Areas of special note include the Clay Avenue shops in Lexington; the shops along MainStrasse in Covington; downtown Shelbyville and Franklin; and Midway's Railroad Street shops (so inviting that the movie *Simpatico* was partially filmed along its sidewalk). In Louisville, tourists and locals alike enjoy visiting the shops and restaurants along Frankfort Avenue and in the Highlands neighborhood.

Established in 1947, this gallery specializes in imported English furniture, fine silver, and works of art. Visitors to the state love to take home sterling silver mint julep cups from Wakefield-Scearce.

))))) **Wakefield-Scearce Galleries**
   525 Washington Street / Shelbyville / 502-633-4382

Clothes and gift shops are just some of the offerings in this historic building anchored by Wakefield-Scearce Gallery and the Science Hill Inn.

))))) **The Shops of Science Hill**
   525 Washington Street / Shelbyville / 502-585-5247

The Image Tree has a great selection of gifts, candles, baby items, frames, and more.

))))) **The Image Tree**
   522 Washington Street / Shelbyville / 502-633-4343

This is where many of the city's chefs shop. Noted by *Louisville Magazine* for their sensual groceries, Creation Gardens stocks exotic oils and grains, elegant dessert shells, and produce to die for—all at wholesale prices.

))))) **Creation Gardens**
   Hancock & Main / Louisville / 502-587-9012

Ambrosia has a wonderfully eclectic selection of gardening and gift items.

))))) **Ambrosia**
   1314 South Virginia Street / Hopkinsville / 270-885-8054

Once an 1840s hotel and tavern, Washington Hall now houses several charming antique, gift, and art shops. Be sure to visit the Marshall Key Tavern while you're there.

))))) **Washington Hall and Marshall Key Tavern**
   2111 Old Main Street / Washington / 606-759-7409

Blue Lamp Gifts is housed in a gracious Victorian row house in historic MainStrasse Village and features gifts, decorative accessories, and homemade fudge.

))))) **Blue Lamp Gifts**
   629 Main Street / Covington / 859-491-3018

Watch as this nationally famous dinnerware and ovenware is made at the Louisville factory. Louisville Stoneware's trademark blue-and-white patterns and gift items are also available in gift shops throughout the state.

))))) **Louisville Stoneware Company**
731 Brent Street / Louisville / 502-582-1900

Edenside Gallery offers an eclectic collection of art and fine crafts, home furnishings, and contemporary and estate jewelry.

))))) **Edenside Gallery**
1422 Bardstown Road / Louisville / 502-459-ARTS

Enjoy a diverse collection of contemporary sculpture, glass, and folk art at either of Swanson Cralle's Galleries.

))))) **Swanson Cralle Gallery**
1377 Bardstown Road / Louisville / 502-452-2904

))))) **Swanson Cralle East Market**
638 East Market Street / Louisville / 502-589-5466

The Gift Box is home of the Candleberry line of candles with names like sugar cookie, blueberry, and key lime that smell good enough to eat. Next door, enjoy lunch or English-style high tea.

))))) **Candleberry Tea Room at the Gift Box**
1502 Louisville Road / Frankfort / 502-875-1111

Located next to the Old Stone Inn, Green Knees Garden Gift Shop is a gift, herb, and garden shop which doubles as a tearoom.

))))) **Green Knees Garden Gift Shop**
6915 Shelbyville Road / Simpsonville / 502-722-5758

COUNTRY STORES AND ROADSIDE MARKETS

Geographers and social historians can debate the question all they want, but we believe that Kentucky's heart is Southern. Why else would the state have so many country stores and farmer's markets?

Located on the banks of the Ohio, Rabbit Hash General Store maintains the flavor and character of the late 1880s, although the merchandise—natural foods, pottery, local art—lends a modern appeal.

))))) **Rabbit Hash General Store**
10021 Lower River Road / Rabbit Hash / 859-586-7744

Located on the Casey/Boyle County border, Penn's is known statewide as the oldest country store in America in continuous ownership and operation by the same family, beginning in 1850 when it was purchased by Gabriel Jackson Penn. Penn's is truly a meeting place, and the owners foster a sense of community by sponsoring readings, celebrations, festivals, and musical performances. Penn's website (they didn't have an outhouse until 1992, but they're already on the web) says, "Impromptu entertainment is not uncommon. At any given time, one may find whittlers, fiddlers, singers, musicians, and storytellers sharing their talents at Penn's Store."

))))) **Penn's Store**
257 Rollings Road / Gravel Switch / 859-332-7715
www.PennsStore.com

Buy plants, fresh produce, gifts, and candy at the year-round market at Red Barn Farms.

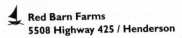 **Red Barn Farms**
5508 Highway 425 / Henderson

Rocky Top Tree Farm & Gifts is the perfect place to browse for trees, fall produce, Kentucky-made crafts, grapevine wreaths, and other handmade accessories for the home.

))))) **Rocky Top Tree Farm & Crafts**
  HC 88, Smiley Basham Road / Hudson / 270-257-2777

Browse for a range of berries and produce, as well as homemade candy, jams, bread, cider, furniture, baskets, and crafts.

))))) **Tower View Farm**
  12523 Taylorsville Road / Louisville / 502-267-2066

The small town of Mt. Sterling has organized a "trading" day for the last two hundred years. One hundred thousand guests from the area enjoy crafts, antiques, food, and music. This charming tradition continues the third Monday in October, including the prior Saturday and Sunday.

▲ **Mt. Sterling Court Day**
  Mt. Sterling / 859-498-5343; 498-8732

WORDS TO LOVE BY

All great lovers are articulate, and verbal seduction is the surest road to actual seduction.—*Marya Mannes*

Kentucky is home to several of the finest independent bookstores in the country. Joseph-Beth Booksellers in Lexington and the three Hawley-Cooke stores in Louisville are both nationally admired full-service booksellers. Carmichael's Books in Louisville has two intimate locations (small spaces and narrow aisles make bumping into your true love all the more likely).

Both Joseph-Beth and Hawley-Cooke host Valentine's Day events for the bookish and love-lorn, and Joseph-Beth has earned a reputation for being the literary equivalent of a singles bar on Saturday evenings.

))))) **Joseph-Beth Booksellers & The Café at Joseph-Beth**
Lexington Green / Lexington / 859-273-2911

The Shelbyville Road location of the Louisville-based chain Hawley-Cooke Booksellers includes **Open Books Café (502-893-0133)**.

))))) **Hawley-Cooke Booksellers**
Shelbyville Road Plaza Center / Louisville / 502-893-0133

))))) **Hawley-Cooke Booksellers**
Glenview Pointe / Louisville / 502-425-9100

))))) **Hawley-Cooke Booksellers**
Gardiner Lane Shopping Center / Louisville / 502-456-6660

One Carmichael's is located next door to **Blue Dog Bakery (502-899-9800)**, a popular Sunday morning stop. The Bardstown branch is attached to **Heine Brothers Coffee and Espresso Bar (502-456-5108)**.

))))) **Carmichael's Books**
2866 Frankfort Avenue / Louisville / 502-896-6950

))))) **Carmichael's Books**
1295 Bardstown Road / Louisville / 502-456-6950

Browse new books at Poor Richard's, then step into the adjacent **Kentucky Coffeetree Café (859-875-3009)** for lunch and more browsing for used books. The Coffeetree hosts first Friday events featuring music and poetry readings.

))))) **Poor Richard's Books**
233 West Broadway / Frankfort / 502-223-8018; 800-730-8018

Located near the University of Kentucky and Woodland Park, Black Swan offers a general selection of collectible and used books with specialties in literature, equine, Kentucky, and military history.

))))) **Black Swan Books**
505 East Maxwell Street / Lexington / 859-252-7255

spotlight

ENJOY ARTS, CRAFTS, AND SPOONBREAD IN BEREA

Berea is regarded as the craft capital of Kentucky, and for good reason. Each spring and fall, the town hosts the Kentucky Guild of Artists & Craftsmen fair at Indian Fort Theater. This outdoor fair offers arts and crafts from over 110 regional artists, as well as demonstrations and musical entertainment. For more information, call **(859) 986-3192**.

Founded in 1855, Berea College is a tiny liberal arts school that provides full-tuition scholarships to all of its students. Eighty percent of its student body comes from the southern Appalachian region and Kentucky, with representation from more than sixty countries. To help finance a portion of their education, Berea students work in a variety of on-campus jobs. Crafts employ nearly two hundred students who work ten to fifteen hours per week learning to make woven goods, pottery, ironworks, woodcrafts, and Shaker-style furniture.

Weaving at Berea began as early as 1896 with Homespun Fairs, which gave parents an opportunity to sell hand-woven items to help raise funds for their children's tuition and board. The fairs were so popular that looms were moved to campus so that the students could learn the craft. Similarly, woodcraft began in the late 1800s when a shop was established as a means to provide tables, chairs and other furniture for students and the campus.

Today, Berea College craft items are available to the public through a catalog (**800-347-3892; www.bereacollegecrafts.com**) and at a variety of gift stores. Two stores in town are devoted to Berea College products:

))))) **Boone Tavern Gift Shop**
   College Square / Berea / 859-985-3137

))))) **Log House Craft Gallery**
   Berea College Campus / Berea / 859-985-3226

In addition, tours of student working studios are possible on weekdays.

Anyone who has strolled along College Square or Chestnut Street, or visited Old Town/Artisans Village knows that Berea College isn't the only reason Berea has been dubbed the Folk Arts and Crafts Capital of Kentucky. The town boasts artisans and artists of every ilk, from quilters and dollmakers, to glassblowers, painters, and jewelers. For a complete listing of Berea's arts and crafts outlets, or for information about studio tours and demonstrations, contact the **Berea Welcome Center (859-986-2540; 800-598-5263, or www.berea.com)**. Note that most of the town's antique shops can be found on either side of Chestnut Street near the town's public buildings.

Located down the street from The Log House Craft Gallery in the College Square shopping district, Churchill Weavers is America's largest and foremost handweaving studio. Free self-guided tours of the studio are available. Churchill items can be found in gift shops, galleries, and boutiques throughout the country and abroad.

))))) **Churchill Weavers**
   100 Churchill Drive / Berea / 859-986-3127
   www.churchill-weavers.com

Established in 1975, the Appalachian Fireside Gallery is located in the block anchored by Boone Tavern. The gallery specializes in a wide range of contemporary and traditional handmade crafts, from furniture and quilts to jewelry and notecards.

))))) **Appalachian Fireside Gallery**
　　127 Main Street / Berea / 859-986-9013

Visit the workshop and showroom of nationally known chair-maker and woodworker Brian Boggs whose beautiful, comfortable Appalachian-style furniture is made without glue or nails.

))))) **Brian Boggs**
　　Lester Street / Berea / 859-986-4638

Take a tour of the workshop of acclaimed craftsman Warren A. May, who makes fine wood furniture and has produced more than ten thousand Appalachian dulcimers so beautiful that many are hung on walls as works of art.

))))) **Warren A. May**
　　110 Center Street / Berea / 859-986-9293

You don't have to stop shopping in Berea just because you get hungry. Hogg Heaven serves up arts, crafts, soups, and sandwiches.

))))) **Hogg Heaven Café & Crafts**
　　210 North Broadway Street / Berea / 859-986-4794

After a long afternoon of shopping in downtown Berea, a cup of coffee or an ice cream cone will hit the spot, or at least tide you over until the next seating at Boone Tavern.

))))) **Berea Coffee & Tea Company**
　　124 Main Street / 859-986-7656 / www.bereacoffee.com

Finally, no visit to Berea would be complete without dinner and an evening at Boone Tavern Hotel. Built in 1909 to house Berea College visitors, Boone Tavern is only one of two inns in the state listed among the National Trust's Historic Hotels of America. Rooms feature elegantly crafted furniture made by student artisans.

Dining at Boone Tavern has been a favorite tradition for Kentuckians and those visiting the Bluegrass State for generations. Trademark dishes include the homemade spoonbread (so beloved it has its own festival every September); Chicken Flakes in the Bird's Nest (pulled chicken in a lightly fried potato "nest"); and a chess pie named for Jefferson Davis, the Confederacy's president who was born at Fairview (then Davisburg) in Todd County. Most of the servers are friendly students working their way through school.

spotlight

ENJOY ARTS, CRAFTS, AND SPOONBREAD IN BEREA

In September, the Berea Spoonbread Festival honors the melt-in-your-mouth cornbread served at Boone Tavern (so-named because it is served with a spoon). The festival features crafts, food, and other activities (**859-986-9760**).

))))) **Boone Tavern of Berea College Hotel**
100 Main Street / Berea / 859-986-9358; 800-366-9358 /
www.historichotels.nationaltrust.org

Love at
First Bite

I think a delicately chosen, artfully presented, lingering, and languorous meal, indulged in publicly, can be one of the most successful fillips to a love affair.

—M. F. K. Fisher, An Alphabet for Gourmets

Nobody wants to kiss when they are hungry.—Dorothy Dix

Kentucky cuisine is essentially traditional Southern cooking. Think biscuits and cornbread, slow-cooked collard greens, home fries, creamed corn, fried apples (sliced apples cooked in a skillet with butter and sugar), and fried chicken (Colonel Harland Sanders opened his first Kentucky Fried Chicken restaurant in Corbin in southeastern Kentucky). Duncan Hines, another Kentuckian who became a household name, was from Bowling Green; every June, the city honors its favorite son with the Duncan Hines Festival, which has events, music, and, of course, food.

Kentucky menus are characterized by a few distinguishing elements: bourbon-flavored everything; delicate Bibb lettuce salad (Bibb lettuce was developed in the state); spoonbread, which Kentucky food writer Ronni Lundy calls "just company cornbread all gussied up in its Sunday best"; Kentucky Hot Brown, a baked dish of ham, turkey, cheese, and bread topped with a white sauce, which originated at the old Brown Hotel in Louisville; and a walnut-and-chocolate chip pie named for the Kentucky Derby.

Given the state's rural/urban split, Louisville, Lexington and the northern Kentucky suburbs of Cincinnati (business types call it the Golden Triangle) boast many of the state's finest eateries. Still, if you crave simple, home-cooked food and aren't afraid of cholesterol or mind dining on Formica tabletops, you can eat well in every region of the state. Romance, like taste, isn't limited to the expensive or fancy. We think this list proves it.

FINE DINING

Kentucky's only five diamond restaurant, The Oakroom is straight out of America's Gilded Age, in what was once the gentlemen's billiards room of this fine old hotel. Executive Chef Jim Gerhardt has searched the state for the finest local meat and produce to incorporate into an exquisite menu: Gethsemani Trappist cheese, made by the monks in Trappist, Kentucky; Colonel Bill Newsom's Aged Gourmet Kentucky Hams (the late food writer James Beard's favorite); Shuckman's smoked fish; locally made sorghum molasses; and Kentucky-raised lamb, ostrich, and free-range chicken. Kentucky bourbon and other fine spirits are selected by the legendary bartender emeritus Max Allen, Jr., who was named 1997 International Bartender of the Year.

))))) **The Oakroom at the Seelbach Hilton Hotel**
500 South Fourth Avenue / Louisville / 502-585-3200

The English Grill, a four-diamond restaurant, has been voted best restaurant for four consecutive years by the *Louisville Courier-Journal*. Chef Joe Castro is known for food with a classical feel but with a strong regional accent. Top off any meal with one of the English Grill's famed dessert soufflés (imagine blackberry soufflé doused in crème anglaise.)

))))) **The English Grill in the Brown Hotel**
335 West Broadway / Louisville / 502-583-1234

Lilly's is a perennial on *Louisville Magazine*'s "best of" lists. "The most influential and celebrated Louisville restaurant of the past decade continues its eclectic, seasonally changing, local produce-loving ways," the magazine says.

))))) Lilly's
1147 Bardstown Road / Louisville / 502-451-0447

Local French favorite Le Relais is located in the Art Deco-style former terminal of Louisville's old airfield. The wood paneling, low lighting, and white tablecloths will make you feel as if you've taken a quick trip to Paris—in the 1920s. If you are looking for a memorable way to propose or celebrate an anniversary, consider purchasing the Romance in the Air package. For an additional $50, you and your love can view the Louisville sunset and other picturesque spots from a two-seat Cessna 172.

))))) Le Relais
Bowman Field / Louisville / 502-451-9020

Located atop a hill in a restored farmhouse in southeast Lexington, Emmett's features regional nouveau cuisine at its finest.

))))) Emmett's
1097 Duval Street / Lexington / 859-245-4444

Don't miss Louisville's version of *Big Night* at Vincenzo's. Owned and operated by brothers Vincenzo (the host) and Agostino (the chef) Gabriele of Sicily, this fine restaurant features traditional Italian cuisine and well-paced meals in a beautiful setting. Details include classical décor, flowers everywhere, and engraved silverware.

))))) Vincenzo's
150 South Fifth Street / Louisville / 502-580-1350

Chez Alphonse is an upscale French restaurant owned by the former maitre d' of Cincinnati's famed Maisonette.

)))))) **Chez Alphonse**
654 Highland Avenue / Ft. Thomas
859-442-5488

An upscale Italian restaurant and imported goods market, Scalea's Ristorante was named Favorite Contemporary Italian restaurant in the 1999 *Cincinnati Magazine* Restaurant Awards. Scalea's deli will put together a picnic basket complete with rented basket and linens for a romantic picnic along the Ohio or Licking Rivers or at Devou Park overlooking nearby Cincinnati.

)))))) **Scalea's Ristorante**
318-20 Greenup Street / Covington
859-491-3334

HISTORIC DINING

Located next to Wakefield-Scearce Galleries in a former girls' school that dates from the early nineteenth century, Science Hill Inn is a great place to dine after a day of shopping in historic Shelbyville. Chef Ellen Gill, trained at the Culinary Institute of America, has created a menu that is both traditional (green beans, cornbread, and biscuits) and contemporary (grilled chicken topped with pineapple salsa, shrimp and grits, and inventive salads). Her fried chicken is regarded as the best in the state.

))))) **Science Hill Inn**
   525 Washington Street / Shelbyville / 502-633-2825

Step back in time when you visit the elegant Beaumont Inn located along tree-lined streets in residential Harrodsburg. The large formal dining room features down-home Kentucky favorites such as two-year-old Kentucky cured country ham; "yellow-legged" fried chicken; Kentucky hot brown; broiled lamb loin chops; and chicken croquettes with cream sauce. Entrees come with plenty of home-style vegetables, and the corn pudding is served family-style.

))))) **Beaumont Inn**
   638 Beaumont Inn Drive / Harrodsburg
   859-734-3381; 800-352-3992 / www.beaumontinn.com

The linen tablecloth spot known as Dudley's serves an inventive menu in an historic schoolhouse near the University of Kentucky. Watch for Kentucky freshwater shrimp in season in September, and be sure to ask for a patio table in spring and fall.

))))) **Dudley's**
   380 S. Mill Street / Lexington / 859-252-1010

Old Talbott Tavern's restaurant, pub, and inn were originally built in 1779 and have been visited by Abraham Lincoln, General Patton, and Jesse James. The restaurant was largely destroyed by fire in 1998 but has reopened after being remodeled.

))))) **Old Talbott Tavern**
   Court Square / 107 West Stephen Foster Avenue / Bardstown
   502-348-3494; 800-4TAVERN

An intimate setting, striking décor (think twinkling lights and leopard-print cushions), and French cuisine make this a staple for Lexington romantics.

)))) À La Lucie
159 North Limestone / Lexington / 859-252-5277

Bistro La Belle and The Depot both make perfect lunch or dinner spots after you've spent the day shopping and antiquing in downtown Midway.

)))) Bistro La Belle
117 East Main Street / Midway / 859-846-4233

)))) The Depot Restaurant
128 East Main Street / Midway / 859-846-4745

The circumstances of owners Chris and Ouita Michel's courtship and marriage—they met as students at the Culinary Institute of America, then returned to her native Kentucky for the wedding and never left—might alone qualify Holly Hill Inn's inclusion in a book about romantic Kentucky. Add to this a cozy restaurant in a historic setting; a seasonal, three-course menu inspired by Ouita's love of authentic cooking traditions and locally farmed products; an expertly selected wine list (Chris is a member of the Guild of Sommeliers); local art adorning walls and tables, and you have a fairy-tale ending to a culinary romance.

)))) Holly Hill Inn
426 North Winter Street / Midway / 859-846-4732

A popular wedding spot, Old Stone Inn was built in the 1700s as a residence and was licensed as a tavern and stagecoach stop from 1826 to 1924, when it reopened as an inn and restaurant. The selection of homemade breads alone (yeast rolls, corn fritters, and warm-water cornbread) are enough to make your mouth water.

))))) **Old Stone Inn**
   6905 Shelbyville Road / Simpsonville / 502-722-8882

Named for Daniel Boone, Daniel's is located on St. Clair Mall in downtown Frankfort.

))))) **Daniel's**
   243 West Broadway / Frankfort / 502-875-5599

Uptown Chatter offers good food in a Victorian Abbey located in the heart of historic Versailles.

))))) **Uptown Chatter**
   160 South Main Street / Versailles / 859-873-1102

Located in the Louisville suburb of Middletown, a twenty-five-minute drive from downtown, Mr. & Mrs. B's Veranda is charmingly situated in an 1890s plantation-style farmhouse. Inside, the Plantation Bar and Lounge offers a selection of 120 different bourbons. Guests who have trouble deciding may sample five for twelve dollars. The Sunday brunch is highly recommended.

))))) **Mr. & Mrs. B's Veranda on Shagbark Hill**
   15206 Shelbyville Road / Louisville / 502-253-0580

Located across from an old mill where Our Best-brand grain products were originally milled and bagged, Our Best Restaurant features old-fashioned cooking and a gift shop located inside the mill.

))))) **Our Best Restaurant**
   5728 Smithfield Road / Smithfield / 502-845-7682

You'll love the elegance of Beehive Tavern's 1790s Colonial row house set on the Ohio River. Enjoy cocktails on the upstairs balcony, or the ever-changing lunch and dinner selections. The Beehive also doubles as a bed-and-breakfast.

))))) **Beehive Tavern**
Main Street and Riverside Drive / Augusta / 606-756-2202

The Back Home Restaurant is locally owned and features regional cuisine in an historic home.

))))) **Back Home Restaurant**
251 West Dixie Avenue / Elizabethtown / 270-769-2800

Visitors to this old schoolhouse can enjoy home cooking while gazing out the windows at the ever-changing foliage near Black Mountain.

))))) **Benham Schoolhouse Inn**
100 Central Avenue / Benham / 606-848-3000

ON THE WATERFRONT

Follow Greenup Street through old Covington, past the row houses and the courthouse, down the incline to the river after River Walk with its larger-than-life statues of Ohio River characters, and you will find an old sternwheeler turned restaurant called Mike Fink. Inside, the main dining area is cozy and provides a marvelous view of the Cincinnati skyline. An attached barge is more spacious and provides a long line of riverside seating with unobstructed views of the river traffic and skyline. It's fun to feel the boat rock from waves churned up by a barge or pleasure boat speeding past. The menu is general and up-to-date, and any taste can be satisfied at what has long been a northern Kentucky dining legend.

))))) **Mike Fink**
Foot of Greenup Street / Covington / 859-261-4212

The celebrated Hall's on the River restaurant continues to serve seafood, sirloin steaks, and its secret recipe beer cheese along the banks of the Kentucky River. General manager David Sidwell reports that during a recent Valentine's Day dinner, thirteen couples became engaged.

))))) **Hall's on the River**
1225 Athens-Boonesboro Road / Winchester / 859-255-8105

The New Orleans-style Whaler's Catch restaurant is located in a restored 1880s building overlooking the confluence of the Ohio and Tennessee Rivers.

Whaler's Catch
123 North 2nd Street / Paducah / 270-444-7701

CASUAL DINING

Lynn's Paradise Café is a fun, funky breakfast and brunch spot with kitschy décor (think fringed lampshades, bright 1950s tables, and mismatched coffee mugs) located in Louisville's Highlands neighborhood.

))))) **Lynn's Paradise Café**
984 Barret Avenue / Louisville / 502-583-3447

Pompilio's Restaurant offers casual Italian fare with competing bocce ball teams in the grass behind the restaurant from April to August.

 Pompilio's Restaurant
600 Washington Avenue / Newport / 859-581-3065

Barbecue, Burgoo, and Other Terms of Endearment

Since Owensboro calls itself the barbecue capital of the world, we would be remiss if we didn't mention a few of the best examples.

Regarded as the best-known barbecue stop in the state, Moonlite has been owned and operated for thirty-five years by three generations of the Bosley family, who still rely on "Pappy's secret recipes."

Moonlite Bar-B-Q Inn
2840 West Parrish Avenue
Owensboro
270-684-8143/800-322-8989
www.moonlite.com

Old Hickory boasts four generations of descendants of Charles Foreman, who first opened the spot in 1918. The Foremans take pride in using all hickory wood. The barbecue is slow cooked

➤

Charlie Brown's, a University of Kentucky hangout, serves casual, inexpensive food and features a warm fireplace, couches, books along every wall, and very dim lighting. It's a great place to warm yourself and someone you love on a cold, rainy night.

 **Charlie Brown's**
816 Euclid Avenue / Lexington / 859-269-5701

ECLECTIC DINING

Located on Covington's MainStrasse at the corner of Sixth Street, Dee Felice Café features New Orleans cuisine, seafood, and jazz every night. House band Sleepcat plays on Fridays and Saturdays. The Dee filet, served blackened and garnished with shrimp cream sauce, is a favorite.

 Dee Felice Café
529 Main Street / Covington / 859-261-2365

The Courthouse Café serves an ever-changing lunch and dinner menu. The restaurant is located across the street from Whitesburg's courthouse and is connected to **The Cozy Corner (606-633-9637)**, a gift shop featuring Appalachian crafts, quilts, and books.

Courthouse Café
Main Street and Webb Avenue
Whitesburg / 606-633-5859

Hopeful romantics and the lovelorn alike can glimpse their romantic futures with the help of tarot card and palm readers every Friday and Saturday evening at Coco's, a well-established and popular jazz club and restarant.

)))) **Coco's**
322 Greenup Street / Covington
859-491-1369

Located just off I-75 on the Tennessee border, the Athenaeum's book-inspired décor and plush seats will please weary travelers.

The Athenaeum
Cumberland Lodge Marriott
649 South Tenth Street
Williamsburg / 606-549-4100

Located in Old Louisville within walking distance of several historic bed and breakfast inns, Buck's signature look includes

(reportedly for twenty to twenty-four hours), basted with a mop, and turned with a pitchfork, just like Grandpa Foreman did.

Old Hickory Barbecue
338 Washington Avenue
Owensboro / 270-926-9000

*In addition, Owensboro hosts the **International Bar-B-Q Festival** downtown each May. Ten tons of barbecued mutton, 5,000 chickens, and 1,500 gallons of burgoo are eaten and judged by the public (502-926-6938; 800-489-1131).*

In case you are wondering what burgoo is, it's a stew made with squirrel (chicken, beef and pork are modern substitutions) and served with barbecue. Although its origins are unclear (similar dishes have been traced to Britain, France, Scotland, and Ireland, as well as to Native American cuisine), Ronni Lundy explains in her book Shuck Beans, Stack Cakes, and Honest Fried Chicken that the stew has become so "ubiquitous around the Bluegrass State at county fairs, political picnics,

➤

lots of white flowers, fine china, and an eclectic menu. For dessert, try their signature mocha dacquoise.

))))) **Buck's**
　　　425 West Ormsby Street
　　　Louisville / 502-637-5284

Woody's Restaurant and Bar invites you to dine amid twinkling lights and an intimate setting.

))))) **Woody's Restaurant & Bar**
　　　246 West Main Street / Richmond 859-623-5130

church socials, and music festivals that it has come to be known as Kentucky burgoo."

*You will definitely want to visit the **Anderson County Burgoo Festival** (502-839-5564) in Lawrenceburg, which pays homage to the stew that is made with "everything but the kitchen sink."*

To sample the best burgoo in the state, Gourmet Magazine columnists and National Public Radio's The Splendid Table's traveling twosome Jan and Michael Stern recommend George's Bar-B-Q in Owensboro.

George's Bar-B-Q
1362 East Fourth Street
Owensboro / 270-926-9276

Housed in three old homes on the Ohio River, this white-tablecloth dining spot has been a local favorite since the early 1900s. Recently remodeled, Caproni's features a Rosemary Clooney room, named for the hometown singer.

))))) **Caproni's Restaurant**
　　　320 Rosemary Clooney Street
　　　Maysville / 606-564-4321

Enjoy seafood, steaks and New Orleans cuisine at the 440 Main Restaurant and Bar in the historic downtown overlooking Fountain Square Park.

🐟 **440 Main Restaurant and Bar**
　　440 East Main Street
　　Fountain Square / Bowling Green
　　270-793-0450 / www.440main.com

Enjoy a casual meal downstairs in The Parakeet Café and Bar, or a finer meal upstairs in The Fletcher House, which features secluded seating, a baby grand piano, and a courtyard with outdoor seating.

The Fletcher House
1129 College Street
Bowling Green / 270-781-1538

Freddie's Restaurant offers fun 1950s décor and classic Italian cuisine.

Freddie's Restaurant
126 South Fourth Street / Danville / 859-236-9884

Stone Hearth Restaurant invites lovers to an evening of fine dining by candlelight.

Stone Hearth Restaurant
1001 North Mulberry Street / Elizabethtown / 270-765-4898

DOWN-HOME AND DELICIOUS

Southern Living magazine is one of the Country Grill's many fans.

The Country Grill
21 Taft Highway / Dry Ridge
859-824-6000

The Star Restaurant is located just twenty-five minutes outside of Louisville in an historic railroad hotel building that time seems to have forgotten. The Star Restaurant isn't fancy, but you'll love the friendly staff and the simple, down-home entrees and vegetables, pancake-style cornbread, and homemade pies and cobblers. A word to the lovelorn: chances are slim that you'll leave The Star without being called "honey" at least once.

The Star Restaurant
401 South Street / West Point / 502-922-4247

Patti's 1880s Settlement is known for its small-town locale, as well as the pork chops, fresh-baked bread with strawberry butter, and their signature Mile-High Meringue Pies. Patti's also has a gazebo that is frequently used for weddings.

Patti's 1880s Settlement
Main Street / Grand Rivers / 270-362-8844; 888-736-2515

Don't expect linen tablecloths at the West End Café, but do expect the best ham biscuit you've ever tasted.

West End Café
2100 West Second Street / Owensboro / 270-686-5939

The family-run Whistle Stop features fried cornbread, down-home vegetables, corn pudding, batter-fried fish, and a variety of cakes and pies made from scratch. Just across the railroad tracks is the **Depot,** which serves up similar tasty cuisine (**201 Jaggers Road / 270-369-6000**).

The Whistle Stop
216 East Main Street / Glendale / 270-369-8586

FUN FOOD

Located in an historic bank building once robbed by Confederate General John Hunt Morgan's troops, Dad's Grill features juke box music, malted shakes, and swivel bar stools in a 1950s-diner style.

Dad's Grill
102 West Main Street / Mt. Sterling

Rockin' Robin Cafe serves burgers, pasta, beef, and ribs as well as an impressive variety of desserts. Owner Vernon Merrick collects

'50s memorabilia and has decorated the establishment with old advertising signs, and museum cases full of toy cars and Howdy Doody memorabilia. Numerous couples have become engaged in a '57 red DeSoto that has been fashioned into a booth. Car lovers will appreciate the '57 pistachio-green Chevy hanging on the wall; a '57 Cadillac that doubles as a hostess station; and the back end of a '59 cotton-candy-pink-finned Caddie that has been fitted with a love seat.

Rockin' Robin Cafe
45 South Highway 27 / Somerset / 606-679-8575

The Bluegrass Grill drive-in has been the site of numerous first glances and first dates. Don't be surprised if you catch Ashland natives Naomi, Wynonna, or Ashley Judd leaning out the window to place an order over the Grill's speakers.

Bluegrass Grill
3505 Winchester Avenue / Ashland / 606-324-3923

Open since 1949, Hill's Barbecue features a big porch, a drive-in window, and an inside counter with nostalgic décor.

Hill's Barbecue
1002 Cuba Road / Mayfield / 270-247-9121

No longer the hot spot it was when it opened in 1951, the Parkette Drive-In will take you back to the days when eating French fries with your steady in the front seat of your dad's Chevy seemed romantic.

Parkette Drive-In
1216 East New Circle Road / Lexington / 859-254-8723

COFFEE, SWEETS AND OTHER TREATS

You'll love this gift shop/gallery/garden shop/herb farm/dessert and lunch spot. The Garden Café features no fewer than nine desserts on its menu, plus several daily specials. Sit near a window and enjoy birds, butterflies, and the garden. Flag Fork also hosts a variety of classes on wreath-making, herbs, and gardening.

))))) **Flag Fork Herb Farm and The Garden Café**
900 North Broadway / Lexington / 859-252-6837

Located in a historic tollhouse, Sweet Surrender serves lunch, but comes to life after dark as a dessert spot. Twenty or so confections, including German chocolate cake, chocolate meringue pie and a towering Granny Smith pie revolve inside an old-fashioned dessert case. Please heed the warning posted on one of the large display cases: "Don't lick the glass!"

))))) **Sweet Surrender**
2311 Frankfort Avenue / Louisville / 502-896-0519

Enjoy homemade ice cream and candies made with old-fashioned care and equipment from Schneider's Homemade Candies.

))))) **Schneider's Homemade Candies**
420 Fairfield Avenue / Bellevue / 859-431-3545

If your sweetie has a sweet tooth, the Homemade Ice Cream & Pie Kitchen's traditional bakery specializing in old-fashioned layer cakes is a must.

))))) **Homemade Ice Cream & Pie Kitchen**
2525 Bardstown Road / Louisville / 502-459-PIES (8184)

If you find yourself turned on by the sight of freshly baked artisan bread, chocolate-filled croissants, or plate-sized cinammon rolls, this stop is a must.

)))) **Bluegrass Baking Company**
      3101 Clays Mill Road / Lexington / 859-296-0581

Visit the 1930 home of Ruth Hunt Candies, the official candy of Churchill Downs and the Kentucky Derby. A traveling minister reportedly named their most famous chocolate, the Blue Monday, claiming that everyone "needed a little sweet to help them through those blue mondays."

◢ **The Hunt Candy Co.**
   426 West Main / Mt. Sterling / 800-927-0302

The birthplace of bourbon candy was founded in 1919 by two women named Rebecca and Ruth. See candy made the old-fashioned way, January through October, and be sure to ask for a free sample.

)))) **Rebecca-Ruth Candy Inc.**
      112 East Second Street / Frankfort
      502-223-7475; 800-444-3766 / www.rrcandy.com

You are invited to tour Old Kentucky Chocolates' kitchen, try a free sample, or shop for chocolate-dipped strawberries (perfect for a romantic picnic) or a basket filled with chocolates, candies, and other Kentucky-made foods.

)))) **Old Kentucky Chocolates**
      450 Southland Drive / Lexington / 859-278-4444; 800-786-0579
      www.oldkycandy.com

Kirchhoff's Bakery, Deli and Market is a fifth-generation bakery located in a historic setting in downtown Paducah.

Kirchhoff's Bakery, Deli and Market
116 Market House Square / Paducah / 270-442-7117

An Amish bakery, Schlabach's serves sourdough bread, sweet rolls, and assorted confections.

Schlabach's Bakery
Highway 181 / Elkton / 270-265-3459

The Tea Cup offers great atmosphere with an antiques store next door.

The Tea Cup
37 East Main Street / Taylorsville / 502-477-0287

Enjoy The Frame Up Gallery's original art, framed prints, and vintage items as you munch on a sandwich.

The Frame Up Gallery Coffee House & Tea Room
1436 Winchester Avenue / Ashland / 606-324-8565

Enjoy coffee and dessert in Planters Coffee House's old, renovated bank building.

Planters Coffee House
130 North Main Street / Henderson / 270-830-0927

spotlight

TEA FOR TWO

Elmwood Inn is the grandmother of all Kentucky tearooms. Guests can enjoy an elegant, four-course affair served on antique silver trays in the 150-year-old inn overlooking the Chaplin River in the Civil War village of Perryville. Open Thursday through Saturday, with seatings at 1 P. M. and 3 P. M. Live music, exhibits by Kentucky artists, and fresh flowers from the inn's gardens add to the ambiance. Be sure to visit the gift shop, which sells tea wares, Elmwood Inn cookbooks, and the Elmwood Inn line of fine teas and gourmet foods.

))))) **Elmwood Inn**
    205 East Fourth Street / Perryville
    859-332-2400; 800-765-2139 / www.elmwoodinn.com

Bruntwood is an antebellum National Register of Historic Places-listed mansion featuring a breathtaking three-story oval staircase. Although Bruntwood is a bed-and-breakfast, anyone with reservations can enjoy the twice-daily luncheon tea served Thursday through Monday.

))))) **Bruntwood Inn**
    714 North Third Street / Bardstown
    502-348-8218; 888-420-9703

On Saturdays, enjoy high tea with your choice of twelve varieties of tea, cucumber sandwiches, and chocolate-dipped strawberries amid the elegant décor of the English Grill in the old-style Brown Hotel.

))))) **The English Grill in the Brown Hotel**
   335 West Broadway / Louisville
   502-583-1234

A shipment of Italian antiques might inspire the chef to add Italian cream cake or Tiramasu to the ever-changing menu.

))))) **Greentree Antiques and Tearoom**
   521 West Short Street / Lexington / 859-455-9660

A Room
with a
View

Romance is a love affair in other than domestic surroundings.—Sir Walter Raleigh

A *listing* of bed-and-breakfast inns in a book about romance speaks for itself. However, if you have any doubts about Kentucky's place in the pantheon of romantic locales, look no further than the state's thriving B&B industry as proof that Kentucky is indeed for lovers.

We've elected to include a representative sample here. For dozens more, the **Bed and Breakfast Association of Kentucky** publishes a wonderful color booklet (**phone 888-281-8188** for copies). We also recommend a visit to the website, **www.bbonline.com/ky/bbak**, which provides a searchable guide to the state's many country and bed-and-breakfast inns

BED-AND-BREAKFAST INNS

The Federal-style Carneal House is ideally situated alongside the Licking River, just one block from the Ohio River in the heart of Covington's Riverside Historic District. Local legend claims that a young woman in gray committed suicide in the house after the visiting General de Lafayette spurned her advances. Today, her ghost is said to make late-night visits.

))))) **The Carneal House**
405 East Second Street / Covington / 859-431-6130

You'll love the antique furniture, sixteen-foot ceilings, and Rococo Revival chandeliers in the 1854 Amos Shinkle House. In an article on Cincinnati, the *New York Times* called it "one of the most beautiful places to sleep in the area."

))))) **Amos Shinkle House**
   215 Garrard Street / Covington / 859-431-2118; 800-972-7012

Looking for lodging that caters not just to you but also the four-legged love of your life? First Farm Inn in northern Kentucky is an animal-friendly bed-and-breakfast that provides boarding for horses and offers riding lessons regardless of skill level (thirty-five dollars per person; make arrangements in advance). The updated 1870s farmhouse is located on a twenty-acre retreat set on the bluffs above the Ohio River, just twenty-five minutes from downtown Cincinnati.

))))) **First Farm Inn**
   2510 Stevens Road / Petersburg / 859-586-0199; 800-277-9527

The French Quarter Inn is idyllically located with a view of the Ohio River.

))))) **French Quarter Inn**
   25 East McDonald Parkway / Maysville / 606-564-8000

The Mullins authentic log-cabin bed-and-breakfast sells herbs, herbal soaps, and gifts. In April, enjoy the Mullins Log Cabin Herb Festival workshops and demonstrations.

))))) **Mullins Log Cabin Country Getaway**
   1435 Denny Road / Berry / 859-824-0565; 888-392-5077

Built in 1792 as a mill, Doe Run Inn is a historic structure made from hand-hewn timber and native limestone. The inn offers a screened porch overlooking Doe Run Creek, park-like grounds, and regional cooking Friday nights and Sunday.

))))) **Doe Run Inn**
      500 Doe Run Hotel Road on KY 448 / Brandenburg
      270-422-2042

Immortalized as the Muhlbach Hotel in F. Scott Fitzgerald's *The Great Gatsby* (the wedding of Daisy Fay and Tom Buchanan was celebrated there), the Seelbach Hilton more recently held the wedding reception for Kentucky lieutenant governor, Steven Henry, and former Miss America (and Maysville native) Heather Renee French. Walk into the hotel's marble, mahogany, and bronze Renaissance Revival lobby and you will realize you have walked into another era. One of many design highlights is the Medieval-looking Rathskeller, a unique setting for special occasions such as wedding receptions and engagement parties. The only room of its kind in the world, the Rathskeller is a work of art made entirely of Rookwood Pottery, which was produced from 1881 until World War II by the famous Cincinnati pottery company. The hotel boasts the state's first and only five diamond dining room, The Oakroom, which was originally a gentleman's billiards room, was once used by Al Capone as a private betting parlor. The completely restored guest rooms feature antique four-poster beds and matching armoires. Weekend packages include romance, horse racing, and the Caesar's River Boat experience. For Kentuckians, the hotel offers a special discounted Hometown Getaway package that includes a free room upgrade to the multi-million dollar concierge level.

))))) **Seelbach Hilton Hotel**
      500 South Fourth Avenue / Louisville / 502-585-3200

The Camberley Brown Hotel, Louisville's premier four-star, four-diamond hotel, is listed in the 2001 edition of *America's Elite 1000*, a guide to the "best purveyors of luxury products and services." You'll love the Brown's opulent, Old World registration desk and lobby, and the Caswell-Massey almond-scented soaps and lotions in the guestrooms.

))))) **Camberley Brown Hotel**
Fourth Street and Broadway / Louisville
502-583-1234; 800-555-8000
www.camberleyhotels.com

Located in the heart of Millionaire's Row in old Louisville, the Samuel Culbertson Mansion was the home of the president of Churchill Downs and the site of numerous Kentucky Derby parties. Two of the Culbertson sons were immortalized in Annie Fellows Johnston's *Two Little Knights of Kentucky,* one of the popular Little Colonel series books for children.

))))) **The Samuel Culbertson Mansion**
1432 S. Third Street / Louisville / 502-634-3100
www.culbertsonmansion.com

You'll love the combination of Old World charm, modern amenities, pampering, and gourmet breakfasts in the Rocking Horse Manor Bed & Breakfast.

))))) **Rocking Horse Manor Bed & Breakfast**
1022 South Third Street / Louisville
502-583-0408; 888-HORSE-BB

The Inn at the Park, a Richardsonian Romanesque mansion, is located in the largest remaining area of Victorian architecture in the United States and is equipped with whirlpools, fireplaces, and in-room phones. Don't miss summer's Shakespeare in the Park performances in the adjacent Central Park, which was designed by Frederick Law Olmsted, the architect of New York's famed Central Park and Atlanta's Piedmont Park.

))))) **Inn at the Park**
1332 South Fourth Street / Louisville
502-637-6930; 800-700-PARK (7275) / www.innatpark.com

The Old Louisville Inn is cited in the 2001 edition of the luxury products and services guide, *America's Elite 1000*.

))))) **Old Louisville Inn Bed & Breakfast**
1359 South Third Street
Louisville / 502-635-1574 / www.oldlouinn.com

Marcardin Inn is a restored cemetery groundkeeper's cottage across the street from Grove Hill Cemetery. Gaze out at resident peacocks over a leisurely breakfast. Just a quarter mile from town, Marcardin nevertheless feels like you are in the middle of nowhere.

))))) **Marcardin Inn**
115 Old Mt. Eden Road / Shelbyville / 502-633-7759

Kentucky's only four-diamond bed-and-breakfast, The Brand House was once the epitome of Federal-style elegance in Lexington and was visited by early socialites and dignitaries including Henry Clay. Conveniently located near downtown, The Brand House gets high marks for breakfast specialties such as Grand Marnier French toast, lemon bread with strawberry butter, and blueberry mousse.

))))) **The Brand House at Rose Hill**
461 North Limestone Street / Lexington
859-226-9464; 800-366-4942 / www.brandhouselex.com

highlight

Spa - aaaah!
Spas and Wellness Getaways

Situated on 1,300 acres of rolling farmland on the Oldham-Jefferson county line, the Wetlands Wellness Spa at Foxhollow is the only destination spa in the state. Foxhollow offers a full range of spa services, including classes in yoga and Pilates, as well as massages, and pedicures, oxygen facials, and LaStone therapy. Overnight accommodations, particularly in the 150-year-old manor house, provide the luxury and amenities of a bed-and-breakfast. Gourmet vegetarian meals are available by reservation at 502-241-8621 or 800-624-7080.

**Foxhollow by the River
609 West Main Street
Louisville / 502-584-3692**

If you are visiting downtown Louisville, enjoy the same services at Foxhollow by the River, a day spa.

**Wetlands Wellness Spa at
  Foxhollow
9601 Covered Bridge Road
Prospect / 502-241-7005**

Listed on the National Register of Historic Places, Gratz Park Inn offers small hotel amenities such as fresh flowers, mahogany four-poster beds and original regional artwork. Perhaps the best amenity is the **Jonathan at Gratz Park** restaurant (**859-252-4949**), which offers one of Lexington's finest dining experiences.

 **Gratz Park Inn
120 West Second Street / Lexington
859-231-1777; 800-752-4166
www.gratzpark.com**

Bed and Breakfast at Sills Inn is a restored Victorian inn filled with Kentucky antiques. *Kentucky Monthly Magazine* readers named this established B&B best in the state.

**Bed and Breakfast at Sills Inn
270 Montgomery Avenue
Versailles
859-873-4478; 800-526-9801
www.sillsinn.com**

Each room in Amelia's Field Country Inn boasts a view of the spectacular Bourbon County countryside. The inn's staff stands ready to provide a picnic basket or plan a historic tour or day at the races. Although the inn's popular restaurant is no longer open year-round, Amelia's Field offers prix-fixe meals for guests and serves meals on a limited basis during the spring and fall seasons.

))))) **Amelia's Field Country Inn**
   617 Cynthiana Road / Paris / 859-987-5778

The Beaumont Inn, a Greek Revival gem, is one of the most popular spots in central Kentucky. Located atop one of Harrodsburg's highest hills (the name means "beautiful mount" in French), the Beaumont Inn features an inviting front porch and grounds furnished with rocking chairs and romantic swings; a first-class restaurant serving classic regional food; a large gift shop; and antiques-filled guest rooms. Be sure to inquire about special packages for the Kentucky Derby, Christmas, and Chef Nick's Cooking School Weekend.

))))) **Beaumont Inn**
   638 Beaumont Inn Drive / Harrodsburg
   800-352-3992; 859-734-3381 / www.beaumontinn.com

The charming Baxter House is an American Four Square home that rests on seven peaceful acres surrounded by cattle, sheep, and horse farms on US 68, one of the most romantic roads in the state. Owners Donna Kirk and GayLynn Gardner have elegantly decorated the spacious rooms, anticipating your every need. Although Shaker Village and Old Fort Harrod State Park are just minutes away, you and your love won't want to leave the comfort of the Navy or Charleston Rooms.

))))) **Baxter House Bed & Breakfast**
   1677 Lexington Road / Harrodsburg
   859-734-4877; 888-809-4457 / www.baxterhouse.com

Visitors arrive at Canaan Land Farm after a seemingly endless mile of winding, gravel road. The house and rooms are romantically rustic, complete with feather tick mattresses on beds just wide enough for two. March and April are popular months because visitors might catch a glimpse of the newborn lambs that populate the farm.

)))) **Canaan Land Farm Bed and
Breakfast
700 Canaan Land Road / Harrodsburg
859-734-3984; 888-734-3984**

The Graystone Manor is located within walking distance of the state Capitol. Special treats are served in the afternoon and evening; dinner is available with special arrangements.

)))) **Graystone Manor Bed & Breakfast
229 Shelby Street / Frankfort
502-226-6196**

The oldest stone manor house west of the Alleghenies, the Old Crow Inn houses Elements Pottery and Crafts, a gift shop that features work by local artisans.

)))) **Old Crow Inn
471 Stanford Road / Danville
859-236-1808**

The Cottage is a favorite honeymoon spot located in a picturesque bluegrass farm setting.

)))) **The Cottage
2826 Lexington Road / Danville
859-236-9642**

Built in 1819 and used as a jail until 1874, it's hard to believe the Jailer's Inn's spacious rooms filled with antiques once housed prisoners. For law-enforcement nuts, however, one guest room still resembles a jail cell and contains two of the original bunks, plus a waterbed. While you're there, you will also want to tour the 1874 jail cells located behind the guest rooms. These cells are listed on the National Register of Historic Places and were part of the state's oldest operating jail complex until it closed in 1987.

))))) **Jailer's Inn Bed & Breakfast**
111 West Stephen Foster Avenue / Bardstown
502-348-5551; 800-948-5551 / www.jailersinn.com

Arbor Rose features an outdoor hot tub/spa and a breakfast terrace overlooking beautifully kept gardens, a koi pond, and fountain. Ask about romance baskets filled with champagne, chocolates, and other goodies, as well as massages available by appointment.

))))) **Arbor Rose Bed & Breakfast**
209 East Stephen Foster / Bardstown
502-349-0014; 888-828-3330
www.arborrosebardstown.com

The Maple Hill Manor, a Kentucky Landmark Home, is listed on the National Register of Historic Places and is considered one of the best preserved in the Commonwealth. A gift shop is located on site. Ask about the Maple Hill Murder Mystery evening, which includes a five-course dinner.

))))) **Maple Hill Manor Bed and Breakfast**
2941 Perryville Road / Springfield
859-336-3075; 800-886-7546

with a king-sized red bed with a heart-shaped headboard as well as a cozy, heart-shaped spa.

Wildwood Inn Tropical Dome & Theme Suites
7809 US 42 / Florence
800-758-2335
859-371-6300
www.wildwood-inn.com

Elihu Lakes House is a renovated log house nestled in the Lakes Creek valley in the Daniel Boone Forest. Guests may fish in the pond, hike, or bring horses to ride along well-kept trails.

Elihu Lakes House
353 Lakes Creek Road / McKee 606-287-7953

The Raintree Inn is located on Lake Cumberland across from Burnside Marina. This Civil War home was featured in the film *Raintree County* starring Elizabeth Taylor and Montgomery Clift (although most of the film was actually filmed in nearby Danville).

Raintree Inn Bed & Breakfast
3314 Old Highway 90 / Bronston / 606-561-5225
www.bbonline/ky/raintree

The Ridge Runner's twenty-room Victorian mansion is situated on a ridge top overlooking the Cumberland Mountains, just minutes from the famed Cumberland Gap, through which Daniel Boone brought Kentucky's first settlers. The absence of modern conveniences, including televisions, stereos, and phones, will leave you with nothing to concentrate on but each other.

Ridge Runner Bed and Breakfast
208 Arthur Heights / Middlesboro / 606-248-4299
www.bbonline.com/ky/ridgerunner/

The Natural Bridge Cabin Country has vacation rental homes overlooking Natural Bridge Resort Area, complete with fireplaces and Jacuzzis.

Natural Bridge Cabin Country
3435 Natural Bridge Road / Slade / 606-663-0283

Located a mile from Renfro Valley Entertainment Center, Brush Arbor is a rustic-looking lodge that sits atop a mountain overlooking a reconstructed Appalachian pioneer village. The village includes a historic church popular for weddings, a picnic spot, and horses for trail riding.

Brush Arbor Bed and Breakfast Inn
Hummel Road / Mt. Vernon / 888-268-4967

According to Paul Thomas at Renfro Valley, Oak Tree Inn's locale is so secluded that "there's nothing to do but fall in love." Sounds good to us.

Oak Tree Inn
1050 Richmond Road / Irvine / 606-723-2600

The Seven Sisters' Inn is actually two historic log cabins joined together and furnished with antiques.

Seven Sisters' Inn
Baptist Road / Campton / 606-668-6444

Nestled in a wood at the top of a hill overlooking Yatesville Lake, the Lake View Hideaway is a modern home that features breathtaking views of the mountains of Kentucky and West Virginia. Guests can enjoy swimming, boating, fishing, and golf at nearby Yatesville Lake. Ask about special occasion, picnic, and romantic baskets. Lunches and dinners are also available.

Lake View Hideaway & Tea Room at Yatesville Lake
Kentucky 1185 / Louisa
606-686-1155; 800-813-1868

Located less than a mile from Carter Caves State Park, the Spanish Manor Inn & Wedding Chapel features beautiful white archways and stained glass windows. Wedding packages range in price from fifty-five dollars (no advance notice necessary; includes two Polaroid photographs and two witnesses) to $1,500. Conveniently, the owner's husband is an ordained minister and a wedding chapel is available on site, as is a pool for summer ceremonies.

The Spanish Manor Inn & Wedding Chapel
US 60 / Olive Hill / 606-286-4141, or 606-286-8593

Kuttawa means "beautiful place" in Shawnee, and this small community near Lake Barkley and Land Between the Lakes boasts no fewer than three bed-and-breakfast hotels. One of them, the Davis House Bed and Breakfast, features spectacular views of Lake Barkley and a private dock where guests can fish, swim, or moor their boats overnight.

The Davis House Bed and Breakfast
528 Willow Way / Kuttawa / 270-388-5585

Located in the heart of Paducah's historic Lower Town, near shopping and museums, the Fisher Mansion is on the National Register of Historic Places.

Fisher Mansion Bed & Breakfast
901 Jefferson Street / Paducah / 270-443-0716

Located on one hundred wooded acres, you'll love the scenic lake and impressive covered porches of the Fox Briar Farm Inn.

Fox Briar Farm Inn
515 Schmidt Road / Paducah
270-554-1774; 888-FOX-BRIAR

The Carriage House Bed and Breakfast will arrange horse-drawn carriage rides through the countryside

The Carriage House Bed and Breakfast
325 Carriage Lane / Madisonville
270-825-8666; 800-536-4503

Relax in the WeatherBerry's charming 1840s farmhouse.

WeatherBerry Bed and Breakfast
2731 West Second Street / Owensboro / 270-684-8760

The Helton House, an early twentieth century Mission-style home, is located in the heart of the tree-lined Buena Vista neighborhood of Owensboro. Enjoy the large front porch and a second-floor sun porch.

Helton House Bed and Breakfast
103 East 23rd Street / Owensboro / 270-926-7117

Dashing Confederate raider John Hunt Morgan is alleged to have ridden his horse up the Myrtledene staircase..

Myrtledene Bed and Breakfast
370 North Spalding Avenue / Lebanon
270-692-2223; 800-391-1721

Romantic
Tours,
Walks, and
Train
Rides

Taking the hands of someone you love,
You see their delicate cages . . .
Tiny birds are singing
In the secluded prairies
And in the deep valleys of the hand.
—Robert Bly, "Taking the Hands"

HISTORIC WALKING TOURS

The Historic Harrodsburg Walking & Driving Tour is one of the most enriching tour guides imaginable. It comes with a glossary of architectural terms.

))))) **Historic Harrodsburg Walking & Driving Tour**
 Harrodsburg / Mercer County Tourist Commission
 800-355-9192

Walk through historic Versailles; drive through Woodford County as you enjoy horse farms and historical landmarks or through Pisgah Historic District, which includes historic homes, ancient trees, and scenic roads.

))))) **Versailles-Woodford County**
 Woodford County Chamber of Commerce
 100 North Main Street / Versailles / 859-873-5122

Tour Lexington's historic areas, including the Gratz Park neighborhood, home to an original Carnegie Library building, Transylvania University, and the homes of Mary Todd Lincoln and Civil War hero John Hunt Morgan.

))))) **Lexington Convention and Visitors Bureau**
 301 East Vine Street / Lexington / 800-845-3959
 www.visitlex.com

Maysville is a historic town situated on the Ohio River. The city loves its history, so be sure to visit the Mason County Museum and the National Underground Railroad Museum during a walking tour of the town's large historic district. While you are in the area, don't miss the eighteenth-century village of Old Washington or nearby Augusta, one of the few Ohio River towns still served by ferry and the hometown of actor George Clooney.

))))) **Maysville Tourism Commission**
216 Bridge Street / 859-564-9411
www.cityofmaysville.com

))))) **Augusta Visitors Center**
116 Main Street / 859-756-2525

Visit nine blocks of historic downtown Louisville or the Victorian neighborhood that hosted the 1880 World's Fair.

))))) **Louisville Main Street Association**
641 West Main / 502-562-0723
Old Louisville Information Center
1340 South Fourth Street / 502-635-5244

From June through August, enjoy a guided tour of more than seventy historic sites in downtown Frankfort, beginning on the lawn of the Old State Capitol.

))))) **Downtown Frankfort Walking Tour**
Frankfort Visitor Center / 100 Capitol Avenue
502-875-8687; 800-960-7200

From the first of June through the end of September, enjoy an evening guided walking tour through Elizabethtown with historic re-enactors representing Jenny Lind, Carry Nation, and General George Armstrong Custer, among others. Walk begins at 7 P. M. Thursdays on the Square. You may also be interested in

Elizabethtown's Historic Driving Tour map, which is available from the tourism and convention bureau.

)))) **Elizabethtown Tourism & Convention Bureau**
1030 North Mulberry / 800-437-0092

A self-guided tour of downtown Richmond features over seventy historic buildings, including three registered national historic districts. The historic downtown, with period lampposts and sixty-five buildings on the National Register of Historic Places, is considered one of the state's finest nineteenth-century commercial districts. A guide book is available for one dollar, plus tax.

)))) **Richmond Downtown Historical Walking Tour**
Richmond Tourism & Visitor Center
345 Lancaster Avenue / 800-866-3705

Enjoy a self-guided tour or a guided introductory bus tour of Historic Bardstown, including Heaven Hill Distillery, June through late August.

)))) **Bardstown Walking Tour & Tourmobile**
Bardstown-Nelson County Tourist Commission
107 East Foster Avenue / 502-348-4877; 800-638-4877

Explore the Downtown Commercial Historic District and four residential neighborhoods of Bowling Green.

Bowling Green Landmark Association
P. O. Box 1812 / Bowling Green / 270-782-0037

The city of Columbia features several historic structures from the late 1700s and early 1800s.

Columbia Tourism Commission
1115 Jamestown Street, Suite 3 / 502-384-4401

Wander through residential and business districts on a two-mile self-guided Ashland Historical Tour.

> **Ashland Historical Tour**
> **Ashland Area Convention & Visitors Bureau**
> **728 Greenup Avenue / 606-329-1007; 800-377-6249**

TENDER IS THE NIGHT

Love doesn't make the world go 'round. Love is what makes the ride worthwhile.—Franklin P. Jones

Lovers everywhere should experience a blue moon in Kentucky at least once in their lives. Here are a few suggestions to get you in the mood, from an old-fashioned ferris wheel on a summer's night to a riverboat dance in the moonlight.

A prototype for the better-known Brooklyn Bridge, this 1886 engineering marvel links Covington to Cincinnati across the mighty Ohio. By day, the Suspension Bridge is a popular footbridge for those on their way to a Reds game. At night, however, the bridge is illuminated by strings of lights and becomes a romantic backdrop for two lovers walking hand-in-hand on a balmy night.

> **John A. Roebling Suspension Bridge**
> **Foot of Second and Court Streets / Covington**

The historic residential area along Riverside Drive, which includes George Rogers Clark Park and the riverwalk, is bordered by the Ohio and Licking Rivers and Fourth Street.

> **Riverside Drive / Licking River National Historic District**
> **Covington**

Dine and dance the night away as you float down the Ohio River with a late night cruise available Friday and Saturday evenings, June through September.

))))) **Dinner Dance and Late Night Cruise**
BB Riverboats / One Madison Avenue / Covington
859-261-8500; 800-261-8586
www.bbriverboats.com

Stroll hand-in-hand along the Ohio River from Fourth to Eighteenth Streets on the Louisville Riverwalk, while you enjoy views of the Ohio, the Portland Canal, and Shippingport Island.

))))) **Louisville's Riverwalk**

Enjoy an early evening cruise and live entertainment on the National Historic Landmark *Belle of Louisville* or *Spirit of Jefferson* as you travel down the Ohio any Tuesday or Thursday evening during the summer.

))))) **Sunset Cruise on the *Belle of Louisville* or *Spirit of Jefferson***
401 West River Road / Louisville
502-574-2355 / www.belleoflouisville.com

Many marriage proposals have been accepted during the Winter Wonderland of Lights annual holiday carriage ride through Ashland's Central Park. For carriage information, contact the Sugarbush Hitch Co. at 800-400-9056. If you are driving, be sure to continue the tour through the surrounding communities of Catlettsburg, Flatwoods, Greenup, Russell, South Ashland, Worthington, and Wurtland.

▲▲ **Winter Wonderland of Lights**
Ashland and surrounding communities

The Southern Lights holiday drive-through light show combines holiday and equestrian themes in one of the most popular tourist events in the region.

))))) **Southern Lights**
   Kentucky Horse Park / 4089 Iron Works Parkway / Lexington
   859-233-4303 / www.kyhorsepark.com

On Saturday evenings from May through the first week in October, downtown Paducah makes room for horse-drawn carriages and dozens of antique show cars. Downtown merchants and restaurants keep their doors open well into the evening as musical groups perform. This glimpse of what downtown was like in the early 1900s draws many local and regional visitors.

⚓ **Paducah's After-Dinner Downtown**

If you and your love need a fright to get your hearts pumping, try the award-winning walking tour, Oak Grove Living History Drama, through historic Oak Grove Cemetery. Every spring and fall, local actors portray cemetery "residents" Irvin Cobb, jazz musician Fate Marabele, and others, who conduct this educational tour by lantern light.

⚓ **Oak Grove Living History Drama**
   P. O. Box 7265 / Paducah
   270-444-8508

A special September hayride tour takes guests through a recreation of the Night Riders of the Black Patch Tobacco War.

⚓ **Night Rider Tour**
   Pennyrile Area Museum / Hopkinsville
   800-842-9959

What could be more romantic than sitting on top of the world with your true love in a fifteen-story-high ferris wheel on a balmy Kentucky evening?

))))) **Giant Wheel at Six Flags-Kentucky Kingdom**
Kentucky Fair and Exposition Center / Louisville
502-366-7508

A January gala, cocktail party, luncheon, and tea party celebrates an exhibition of artist-made dinnerware at Percy Brown Hall at the historic Water Tower. Opening the exhibition is the DinnerWorks Gala, a black-tie affair catered by some of the area's best-known chefs. Table designs are extravagant, and guests dress in costume to complete the theme.

))))) **DinnerWorks**
Louisville Visual Art Association / 3005 Upper River Road
Louisville / 502-896-2146

The Café Kilimanjaro features a dance floor and live reggae, African, Latin, and other world music.

))))) **Café Kilimanjaro**
649 South Fourth Street / Louisville
502-583-4332

The Rudyard Kipling restaurant/bar is home to a variety of small local theatre groups as well as local jazz, folk, rock, and Bluegrass musicians. Monday evening is Dark Night Theatre night at the Rudyard Kipling, because most live theaters and restaurants in town are closed. Wednesday evenings feature jazz jam sessions.

))))) **The Rudyard Kipling**
422 West Oak Street / Louisville
502-636-1311

Stop by the Shepherdsville Country Music Place for a Bluegrass Friday Night with regional bands or the occasional visiting luminary.

))))) **Shepherdsville Country Music Place**
Shepherdsville / 502-969-3515

Enjoy jazz in a Jazz Age setting at Old Seelbach Bar for weekday happy hour or late-night weekend evenings.

))))) **Old Seelbach Bar**
500 South Fourth Avenue / Louisville / 502-585-3200

If you are visiting Kentucky during Halloween, note that many of the state's historic sites, including White Hall; Ashland, the Henry Clay Estate; and Old Fort Harrod State Park offer "ghost walks" of the areas' haunted sites and spooky happenings to celebrate the season.

STRANGERS ON A TRAIN

With its natural beauty and historic landscape, Kentucky is the perfect place to fall in love or rekindle a romance while you enjoy a leisurely train ride. Here are a few of our favorites:

Eat lunch or a four-course, white-tablecloth dinner on a historic train that travels the route of the old Louisville & Nashville railroad through Limestone Springs and the Bernheim Forest. The two-and-a-half-hour excursion on My Old Kentucky Dinner Train is a romantic way to ring in the New Year or celebrate Valentine's Day. The train also offers special mystery dinner rides.

))))) **My Old Kentucky Dinner Train**
602 North Third Street / Bardstown / 502-348-7300
www.kydinnertrain.com

The Bluegrass Scenic Railroad offers a ninety-minute excursion through the rolling hills and picturesque farmland that typifies the Bluegrass region. Special events include Halloween and Christmas rides and a Civil War Drama and Train Robbery with a reenactment performed by the Fifth Texas Mounted Volunteers. Coach rental is also available for birthdays, weddings, or a private rendezvous for two.

))))) **Bluegrass Scenic Railroad**
US Hwy 62 / Woodford County Park / Versailles
859-873-2476; 800-755-2476

Part of the Big South Fork River and Recreation Area, the namesake railway takes visitors back to a time when coal was king. The train travels through land once occupied by loggers and miners, hugging cliff lines and following mountain streams as passengers descend over six hundred feet in five miles to the floor of the Big South Fork River valley.

▲ **Big South Fork Scenic Railway**
P. O. Box 368, 21 Main Street / Stearns
800-GO-ALONG (800-462-5664)

The Kentucky Railway Museum offers a seventeen-mile excursion between New Hope and Lebanon Junction on Old No. 152, a 1905-vintage steam locomotive, which historians believe was used to pull one of Theodore Roosevelt's presidential campaign trains and the car that transported Al Capone to prison.

))))) **Kentucky Railway Museum**
P. O. Box 240 / New Haven / 502-549-5470; 800-272-0152
www.kyrail.org

Jonesie's Overland Stagecoach offers old-fashioned hay rides, stagecoach, and carriage rides in all sizes and styles, as well as tours of Historic Bardstown seven days a week.

)))) **Round the Town Carriage & Stagecoach**
Jonesie's Overland Stagecoach
223 North Third Street / Bardstown / 502-348-0331

Tour historic Paducah from one of Annie's Horsedrawn Carriages.

Annie's Horsedrawn Carriages
Second and Broadway / Paducah / 888-4ANNIES

The Rivertown Carriage Co. regularly departs from Fifteenth Street and Winchester, Thursday through Saturday, and also offers weekend historical, romantic, and storytelling rides.

Rivertown Carriage Co.
2929 Forgey Street / Ashland / 606-329-0417

The Meadowbrook Farm cattle, swine, and sheep farm provides hayrides on request.

)))) **Meadowbrook Farm**
Meadowbrook Road / Richmond / 859-369-5426

Enjoy a three-hour tour of the Louisville metropolitan area from Joe and Mike.

)))) **Joe & Mike's Pretty Good Tours**
3744 Glenmeade Road / Louisville / 502-459-1247

Visit the best of Louisville's downtown, with its museums, theaters, and riverfront; the eclectic Highlands neighborhood shops and restaurants; and Frankfort Avenue, home to the Clifton and

Crescent Hill neighborhoods, as well as many art galleries, bookstores, coffee shops, and restaurants. The trolley runs Saturdays from late August through October.

))))) **Louisville Trolley Hop**
    1000 West Broadway / Louisville / 502-585-1234

Stage a memorable proposal, or just get swept off your feet during a one-hour balloon ride.

))))) **Crawford Hot Air Balloons, Inc.**
    1812 Foxboro Road / La Grange / 800-242-2966
    502-222-7600

spotlight

KENTUCKY STRAIGHT
Bourbon Culture in Kentucky

Many Kentuckians believe that an afternoon spent sipping a bourbon-laced mint julep on the terrace at Churchill Downs on Derby Day is the height of romance. While the sweet cocktail doesn't suit everyone's tastes, and the finery of Millionaire's Row may be beyond your means, the history and culture of this Kentucky original is accessible to everyone.

Although the earliest distillery is difficult to determine, Kentucky lays claim to being the homeplace and world's favorite producer of America's only native spirit. The name bourbon likely came from Bourbon County, Kentucky, where several early distillers were located. Today, as much as ninety-five percent of the world's bourbon is produced in the state, and Maker's Mark, with its signature red wax-tipped bottle, is regarded by bartenders, restaurants, and enthusiasts around the world as a bourbon without peer.

Many local distilleries offer free historic and educational tours. Romance-seekers take note: a visit to a Kentucky bourbon distillery is sure to stimulate all of the senses, from the aroma of bubbling yeast and grain and the shine of copper pots to the bourbon-soaked darkness of a barrel-aging warehouse. You'll also learn the meaning of terms such as "white dog" (the distilled bourbon before it has acquired its dark color from aging in a charred oak barrel) and the "angel's share" (the five percent of the bourbon that evaporates during the aging process).

Couples unfamiliar with bourbon culture can gain a quick education by participating in the Bourbon Festival in Bardstown or taking a bourbon-themed train ride through the Kentucky countryside. For history buffs and bourbon connoisseurs alike, tours offered by Maker's Mark and Labrot & Graham National Historic Landmark distilleries are must-sees.

No visit to Kentucky is complete without a visit to Maker's Mark's famed distillery. Enjoy the grounds, and be sure to dip your own souvenir bottle in wax during a visit to the gift shop.

))))) **Maker's Mark**
3350 Burks Springs Road / Loretto / 502-865-2099
www.makersmark.com

Marvel at the Labrot & Graham distilling room from 1840, which uses copper-pot stills and is the only surviving stone aging warehouse left in America. It's filled floor to ceiling with fragrant barrels of bourbon.

))))) **Labrot & Graham**
7855 McCracken Pike / Versailles / 859-879-1939
www.l-g.com

Visit Heaven Hill, the world's largest independent, family-owned producer and marketer of distilled spirits and the second largest supply of aging bourbon in the world.

))))) **Heaven Hill**
1064 Loretto Road / Bardstown / 502-348-3921

Visit Leestown Company and Buffalo Trace Distillery, America's largest distillery and the home of Ancient Age, the Single Barrel Bourbon Society, and such popular single-barrel bourbons as Buffalo Trace, Blanton's, Rock Hill Farms, Hancock's Reserve, and Elmer T. Lee.

))))) **Leestown Company and Buffalo Trace Distillery**
1001 Wilkinson Boulevard / Frankfort
502-223-7641; 800-654-8471 / www.buffalotrace.com

The Jim Beam American Outpost's tour film *American Spirit* features sixth-generation master distiller emeritus Booker Noe, grandson of Jim Beam. The Jim Beam Nature Preserve provides picturesque views of the Kentucky River, marked trails, prairie patches, and caves, and is home to rare species of plant and animal life.

))))) **Jim Beam American Outpost**
149 Happy Hollow / Clermont / 502-543-9877

Austin Nichols is the home of Rare Breed and Wild Turkey, which carry the slogan "101 proof, real Kentucky."

))))) **Austin Nichols**
US Hwy 62 East / Lawrenceburg / 502-839-4544

Four Roses is located in an unusual California Spanish Mission-style building from 1910.

))))) **Four Roses**
1224 Bonds Mill Road / Lawrenceburg / 502-839-3436

Enjoy tours, entertainment, barrel racing, and dinner on the My Old Kentucky Home Dinner Train, the Kentucky Railway Museum Bootleggers Train Robbery, and, of course, bourbon tasting at the festival which celebrates Kentucky as the Bourbon Capital of the World.

))))) **Kentucky Bourbon Festival**
   P. O. Box 867 / 107 East Stephen Foster Avenue / Bardstown
   502-348-4877; 800-638-4877

The Kentucky Distillers Association provides the color brochure and map "Kentucky Bourbon Trial," which highlights every distillery tour in the state.

))))) **Kentucky Distillers Association**
   110 West Main Street / Springfield / www.kybourbon.com

))))) **Oscar Getz Museum of Whiskey History**
   Spalding Hall / 114 North Fifth Street / Bardstown
   502-348-2999

Things to Do on a Rainy Day

Love vanquishes time. To lovers, a moment can be eternity, eternity can be the tick of a clock.—Mary Parrish, All the Love in the World

Don't let a scorching summer's day or a rain shower

deter your plans for romance; just relocate your beloved indoors. Historic homes can take you and your partner to another era and way of life, or a planetarium can take you to another planet altogether.

BEST BETS

"The Bizarre, the Beautiful, the Dangerous and the Deadly . . ." No, this isn't some oversexed soap opera—it's a description of what awaits you at the Newport Aquarium. The pride of Newport, once a haven for organized crime and gambling, this new attraction features more than 11,000 fish and six hundred species of underwater creatures as you wander through two hundred feet of clear, seamless acrylic viewing tunnels. Highlights include the tranquil music and lighting of the Jellyfish Gallery; "the bizarre and beautiful" exhibit of exotic water creatures; and "the dangerous and deadly" collection of sharks. See if your love doesn't draw a little closer when he or she is surrounded by a 380,000-gallon tank full of deadly sharks.

))))) **Newport Aquarium**
One Aquarium Way / Newport / 859-491-FINS; 800-406-FISH
www.newportaquarium.com

Also located in northern Kentucky, the hundred-year-old Cathedral Basilica of the Assumption houses the world's largest handmade stained-glass window as well as canvas murals painted by Covington artist Frank Duveneck. Pope Pius XII recognized the cathedral as a minor basilica in 1953, one of only thirty-five in the United States.

))))) **The Cathedral Basilica of the Assumption**
1140 Madison Avenue / Covington

HISTORIC HOMES

It's difficult to avoid getting caught up in the romance of an old house, particularly when its inhabitants led unusual or remarkable lives. Here are a few Bluegrass homes we recommend you visit:

Located in one of Lexington's oldest and finest neighborhoods, the Henry Clay Estate's Italianate mansion stands on the site of the original Ashland, home to the Great Compromiser and three-time presidential candidate Henry Clay. The interior of the house has been restored to its 1880 appearance and features Clay family art and furniture. Outbuildings on display include a smokehouse, a privy, icehouses, and a dairy cellar. Clay's 1833 carriage is also on view.

Though not large, this historic home offers a jewel of a walled garden, filled with boxwood, herbs, perennials, and heavenly scented gardenias. The surrounding twenty-acre grounds are white with tiny wildflowers in the spring and make a great spot for walking hand-in-hand or for a romantic picnic for two. Be sure not to miss the peony garden in which rows and rows of pink, red, and white old-fashioned peonies burst forth in May splendor.

While you're visiting Ashland, dine outdoors at the **Ginkgo**

Tree Café (859-266-8581), which features a limited menu of gourmet sandwiches, desserts, tea, and lemonade served April through October, weather permitting.

)))))) **Ashland: The Henry Clay Estate**
    120 Sycamore Road / Lexington / 859-266-8581

Built by Daniel Boone's nephew and namesake, Daniel Boone Bryan, Waveland plantation provides a step back in time to mid-nineteenth-century Kentucky. The home takes its name from the acres of grain and hemp "waving" in the breeze. Guests are invited to use the picnic tables and playground on the grounds. Christmas at Waveland is a candlelit tour with period decorations and music, refreshments, and a visit by members of the Bryan "family."

)))))) **Waveland State Historical Site**
    225 Higbee Mill Road / Lexington / 859-272-3611

Home of abolitionist Cassius Marcellus Clay, the forty-four room White Hall State Historic House displays original and period antiques, a restored cookhouse, and outside slave quarters. Enjoy a romantic meal at White Hall's shaded picnic area.

)))))) **White Hall State Historic House**
    500 White Hall Shrine Road / Richmond
    859-623-9178

Once the home of John Brown, Kentucky's first senator, Liberty Hall dates from the state's first decade and is decorated with local antiques owned by four generations of the Brown family. The nearly three acres of grounds includes beautiful perennial and annual borders and the largest formal boxwood garden in the state.

)))))) **Liberty Hall Historic Site**
    218 Wilkinson Street / Frankfort / 502-227-2560

Standing atop a gentle rise overlooking the Ohio (in fact, the front door opens onto the great river), the Farnsley-Moremen House is a classic two-story, brick I-shaped house with a Greek Revival full-height portico. Visitors can tour this historic home and grounds and enjoy ongoing seasonal excavations and a kitchen garden. A modern boat landing allows visitors to take an excursion on the *Spirit of Jefferson,* a replica paddlewheeler, from July through October.

))))) **Riverside, The Farnsley-Moremen Landing**
7410 Moorman Road / Louisville / 502-935-6809

Located near a bluff overlooking the Ohio River, the Locust Grove Historic Home from the eighteenth century was the last residence of George Rogers Clark. The home, including the gardens and outbuildings, have been lovingly restored. We know of at least one couple who was married at Locust Grove and who return annually for an anniversary dinner on the lawn.

))))) **Locust Grove Historic Home**
561 Blankenbaker Lane / Louisville / 502-897-9845

Visit the Federal-style house that inspired Stephen Foster's ballad, "My Old Kentucky Home." During the Christmas season, horse-drawn carriages, boarded in the town square, carry you to the candlelit mansion for an evening tour.

))))) **Federal Hill**
501 East Stephen Foster Avenue / Bardstown
502-348-5551; 800-323-7803

The Riverview at Hobson Grove is a fine Italianate mansion interpreted to the 1860s–1890s and the structure and its furnishings represent those of a prosperous Victorian family living in south central Kentucky.

Riverview at Hobson Grove
1100 West Main Avenue / Bowling Green / 270-843-5565

The Adsmore Museum from 1857 annually hosts a recreation and celebration of the 1907 engagement and marriage of one of the home's former residents, Selina Smith, to Dr. John Osborne, former governor of Wyoming. View bridal items and gifts, as well as Selina's wedding dress and bridal trousseau as you step back into the world of a wealthy early-twentieth-century family in western Kentucky.

Adsmore Museum
304 North Jefferson / Princeton / 270-365-3114

Even the name of this site is romantic. Mimosa Mansion is said to be the largest single-family home in northern Kentucky.

Mimosa Mansion Museum
412 East Second Street / Covington / 859-261-9000

HISTORIC AND CULTURAL SITES

Who wouldn't get a little excited by roomfuls of pure gold? Known as the Gold Vault, the United States Treasury Department Gold Depository is a granite structure built in 1936 and contains a two-level vault with a door weighing more than twenty tons. Unfortunately, no visitors are allowed to enter, and the vault is guarded twenty-four hours a day.

United States Treasury Department Gold Depository
Gold Vault Road / Fort Knox

The Kentucky History Center's permanent exhibit takes visitors on a walk through Kentucky's history, including life-size environments and interactive displays. The museum also contains space for traveling exhibits, a research and reading library, special collections study room, and spaces for films, lectures, and other events.

))))) **Kentucky History Center**
100 West Broadway / Frankfort
502-564-1792
www.kyhistory.org

In Love and War
Johnse Hatfield and
Roseanne McCoy

Pikeville in eastern Kentucky is a key site in the storied feud between the Hatfields and McCoys. Like their predecessors the Capulets and Montagues, the Hatfields and McCoys produced a pair of star-crossed lovers. During the election season of 1880, Johnse Hatfield, son of Devil Anse Hatfield, a Confederate who killed Union sympathizer Harmon McCoy, traveled from West Virginia to Kentucky. The Kentucky elections grounds was a social gathering place for mountain people, and it was there that

➤

The Kentucky Museum and Library houses a rich collection of exhibits which enables visitors to revisit the past and learn about the state's history and heritage.

🖙 **Kentucky Museum and Library**
Western Kentucky University
1 Big Red Way / Bowling Green
270-745-2592

Fifty-six steps—one for each year of his life—lead to a granite temple enshrining President Lincoln's natal cabin at the Abraham Lincoln National Historic Site.

))))) **Abraham Lincoln National**
Historic Site
US 31 East South / Hodgenville
502-358-3874

The Black History Gallery's collection includes photographs, articles, biographies, and other memorabilia depicting the history and cultural heritage of African Americans.

))))) **Black History Gallery**
  602 Hawkins Drive / Elizabethtown
  502-769-5204; 502-765-7653

Appalshop is a Kentucky gem and a haven for Appalachian writers, singers, and filmmakers and includes a gallery, a music and video store, and video and music production facilities. Each June Appalshop hosts the Seedtime on the Cumberland Festival, which showcases traditional Appalachian musicians, storytellers and artists, as well as the Hillbilly Nation rock and blues celebration in Wise, Virginia.

Every month or so, the people of Appalshop organize a Carcassonne Dance, a traditional square dance, complete with a caller and a live band held at the local Carcassonne Community Center. Intricate contra line dances are the order of the evening, but even if you just watch, it's a great way to experience a part of native Kentucky heritage.

Appalshop
  19 Madison Avenue / Whitesburg
  606-633-0108
  www.appalshop.org

Johnse met a red-headed Kentuckian named Roseanne McCoy. The two fell in love and planned to marry, despite the objections of Devil Anse. During a rendezvous with Roseanne at the home of her aunt, however, Johnse was taken prisoner by McCoy kinsmen. Knowing that her beloved would be murdered at the first opportunity, Roseanne borrowed a neighbor's horse and rode to Devil Anse for help. The McCoy posse was stopped, but Johnse never risked seeing Roseanne again. Sadly, the brief union led to tragedy. A Hatfield-McCoy daughter, Sarah Elizabeth, was born in 1881 and died within a few months from the measles. Roseanne died alone at the age of thirty.

Located at Hidden River Cave, the American Cave Museum show-cases the state's underground natural history through numerous exhibits.

American Cave Museum
119 East Main Street / Horse Cave / 270-786-1466

A great wedding site, the Behringer-Crawford house sits on top of a hill with terraced gardens and a screened back porch. The collection houses archaeological finds and other historic artifacts, as well as fine and folk art.

Behringer-Crawford Museum
1600 Montague Road / Devou Park / Covington
859-491-4003

The Crane House and Asia Institute hosts lectures, workshops on such diverse topics as Mandarin language and bonsai gardening, cooking, storytelling, and other educational programming related to Asian history and culture.

The Crane House / Asia Institute
1244 South Third Street / Louisville / 502-635-2240

Site of the first wedding in Kentucky, the Fort Boonesborough historic site features a reconstructed fort of Daniel Boone's establishment in which pioneer crafts are demonstrated using functioning antiques from the eighteenth century.

Fort Boonesborough State Park
KY 627 / Richmond / 859-527-3131

Mountain HomePlace on Paintsville Lake in eastern Kentucky features five original nineteenth- and early-twentieth-century structures that have been relocated from the surrounding area. A visitor's center houses a museum and a gift shop with eastern Kentucky crafts. The first weekend in October, the HomePlace comes alive for the annual harvest, when visitors can witness the making of sorghum and other traditional farm ways.

Mountain HomePlace
P. O. Box 1850 / Staffordsville / 606-297-1850

A NIGHT AT THE MOVIES

Sometimes, you just want to hold hands in the dark. The movie date is a staple couple's outing, and it's a good way to ease into the early stages of a new relationship. You don't need this book to find your local Movies 10, but there are several historic movie theaters around the state offering an evening out in grand style. Or why not indulge in a little nostalgia and rekindle your love under the stars at a drive-in theater?

The Kentucky is a stunningly restored silent movie palace that shows first run and art films. Right next door, the State Theater is an absolute jewel. This smaller theater is painted to make you feel as if you've stepped into an Italian courtyard, complete with balconies, soft lighting, and winking stars overhead.

The Kentucky Theatre
The State Theatre
214 East Main Street / Lexington / 859-231-6997

A trip to the drive-in has the makings of a nostalgic jaunt for some, an exciting new experience for others. It's all there—wide open sky, a big screen, and you and your date alone in a car. Need we say more?

Chakers Skyvue Drive-In
Rt. 60 / Winchester / 800-4 SKYVUE

🐟 **Sky-View Drive-In**
Celina Road / Tompkinsville / 502-487-5359

🐟 **Drive-In Theatre**
6250 Nashville Road / Franklin / 502-586-1905

The films shown on the multi-story IMAX screen at the Louisville Science Center will take your breath away. With subjects ranging from the Great Pyramids to volcanoes to Mount Everest, you'll experience the sensations of flying, falling, and the wonder of the majesty of the natural world.

))))) **IMAX Theater at the Louisville Science Center**
727 West Main Street / Louisville / 502-561-6100

STARRY, STARRY NIGHT: PLANETARIUMS

Hey, it's dark in here. What more could you want? Planetariums make a great—and very romantic—outing.

Think of Woody Allen and Diane Keaton in *Annie Hall,* or James Dean and Natalie Wood in *Rebel Without a Cause,* and you'll get the picture. It's no wonder so many romantic movies are set inside planetariums. Planetariums enable you to travel to the stars without leaving the comfort of your seat, and informative planetarium shows will let you experience some of the many wonders of the universe.

Eastern Kentucky University's Hummel Planetarium and Space Theater is the third largest planetarium in the world located on a college campus. Shows will project up to ten thousand stars, and you can view the night sky as it would appear from any point on the earth at any time. The dome onto which images are projected in the theater's Space Voyager Planetarium is tilted twenty-seven degrees and is 67.5 inches in diameter, making it one of only four of its kind in the world.

))))) **Hummel Planetarium and Space Theater**
Kit Carson Drive / Eastern Kentucky University / Richmond
859-622-1547

Stargazers at the Golden Pond Planetarium and Observatory won't want to miss the periodic Star Parties and public observing sessions, hosted by the West Kentucky Amateur Astronomers. The planetarium is open to the public March through December.

The Golden Pond Planetarium and Observatory
Golden Pond Visitor's Center
Land Between the Lakes National Recreational Area
270-924-2000

The Hardin Planetarium has a forty-foot dome housing a Spitz A3P star projector and various special-effects projectors. Public lectures are designed to be educational and entertaining.

Hardin Planetarium
Western Kentucky University
Department of Physics and Astronomy / Bowling Green
270-745-4044

Other places you and your special someone could wish upon a shooting star include:

))))) **Gheens Science Center and Rauch Planetarium**
University of Louisville, Belknap Campus / Louisville
502-852-6664

))))) **Berea College Weatherford Planetarium**
Science Building / Berea / 859-985-3351

Romantic Getaways

With its diversity of landscapes, culture, and activities, Kentucky is the perfect setting for an impromptu daytrip spent antiques-hunting, a celebratory weekend of fine dining and cultural activities, or a week-long vacation spent hiking, sailing, fishing, and swimming. While we hope you will use this book to plan your own Kentucky adventure based on your (and your partner's) romantic interests, listed below are some concrete suggestions for a weekend spent enjoying the state and each other.

Frankfort has put together a Romantic Getaway weekend package that includes a garden stroll behind Liberty Hall; a carriage ride through historic downtown Frankfort; a drive along Old Frankfort Pike; dining at Daniel's downtown or overlooking the Kentucky River at Jim's Seafood; and lodging in one of the area's bed-and-breakfasts or hotels. Couples visiting the area may also be interested in other getaway packages that feature rafting down the Elkhorn Creek's whitewater gorge; hiking along Red River Gorge; bird-watching and kayaking or canoeing with a professional guide; touring historic sites; and learning about African-American history and culture or the state's bourbon heritage.

 Frankfort-Franklin County Tourist & Convention Commission
Frankfort / 800-960-7200 / www.frankfortky.org

The Quilt City USA Get-A-Way package includes two nights at a local bed-and-breakfast, local dining, nine hours of quilting classes led by nationally recognized teachers, tours, and shopping in historic downtown Paducah.

 Quilt City USA Get-A-Way
Paducah-McCracken County Convention & Visitors Bureau
P.O. Box 90 / Paducah / 800-723-8224

spotlight

SIMPLE PLEASURES
Shakers in Kentucky

The peculiar grace of a Shaker chair is due to the fact that it was made by someone capable of believing that an angel might come and sit on it.

—Thomas Merton

Kentucky is blessed with two restored Shaker Villages, one in Harrodsburg at Pleasant Hill in central Kentucky, and the other at South Union in western Kentucky a few miles west of Bowling Green. Both village sites are listed on the National Register of Historic Places and provide an ideal locale for a romantic weekend, especially if your objective is to share quiet moments or luxuriate in tranquility.

Shakers were a peaceful, practical, hard-working people who believed in equality. Their quest for simplicity and perfection, coupled with their innovative and practical designs has led to the term "Shaker-made" to stand as a mark of excellence in design and craftsmanship. The Shakers also practiced celibacy, which in some regards is antithetical to the purpose of this book. However, we find that the simple beauty and serenity of the Shaker landscape and culture might be the perfect antidote to what ails many modern romances, including stress, overwork, and saturation of media and commerce.

Shakers came to central Kentucky in 1805, establishing Pleasant Hill Village on a high plateau above the Kentucky River near Harrodsburg. By the mid-nineteenth century, the community was thriving and included as many as five hundred residents. By 1910, however, only a few Shakers remained and the village was closed.

spotlight

SIMPLE PLEASURES
Shakers in Kentucky

Today, thirty-three original buildings have been restored and 2,700 acres of farmland preserved at Pleasant Hill. It is the only site of its kind where all visitor services are provided in original buildings, and is the largest historic community of its kind in America. Visitors can view original Shaker furniture and enjoy exhibits, crafts stores, dining and overnight accommodations in restored nineteenth-century buildings.

Pleasant Hill's riverboat, the *Dixie Belle*, is an authentic sternwheeler and the only vessel offering public excursions on the Kentucky River along the scenic palisades, where you'll marvel at high limestone cliffs and High Bridge, an engineering wonder when it was built in 1877.

From April through October, enjoy seminars on native flora, fauna, geology, and architecture conducted—frequently aboard the *Dixie Belle*—by educators from local schools and universities. You can also enjoy workshops on such topics as nineteenth-century farming, Shaker chairmaking, herbs, heirloom vegetable gardening, basketry, and rug hooking.

 Shaker Village of Pleasant Hill
3501 Lexington Road / Harrodsburg
859-734-5411; 800-734-5611 / www.shakervillageky.org

The Shaker community at South Union was founded in 1807, and once sprawled across six thousand acres and two hundred buildings. Today, only three of the original buildings remain. The 1824 Centre House offers guided tours of schoolrooms, sleeping quarters, dining rooms, and a kitchen, as well as rooms once dedicated to sewing, laundry, woodworking, broom making, and food preserving, all filled with original Shaker furnishings and artifacts.

Shaker Museum at South Union
850 Shaker Museum Road / South Union / 270-542-4167
800-811-8379 / www.logantele.com/~shakmus/

While you're visiting South Union, be sure to schedule a stay at the Shaker Tavern, an 1869 hotel located in the commercial district of South Union Shaker Village and built to cater to Victorian-era railroad travelers. Modern-day romance-seekers will find it to be a gem in an appealingly secluded locale.

Originally built as a business venture by the South Union Shakers to house a hotel for traveling "foreigners," or non-Shakers, the Shaker Tavern is located steps from the old train depot, but feels like the middle of nowhere. Actually, the tavern is conveniently located ten miles west of Bowling Green and forty-five minutes north of Nashville, Tennessee. Breakfast includes the lightest, most tender biscuits found inside or outside the state. Highly recommended.

The Shaker Tavern
Highway 73 / South Union / 270-542-6801; 800-929-8701

Visit a gentle people who lead full lives with no electricity or gas-powered machines. Fresh produce, molasses, and homemade goods in a setting of well-tended farmland makes this a satisfying destination.

Mennonite Community
KY 100 / 585 and KY 1333 / Allen County

Visit an Amish Community, enjoy antiques, cultural and historical sites, and museums as a part of the Back Roads Tour.

Back Roads Tour
Crittenden County / 270-965-2418

Arts
for the
Heart

The more I think about it, the more I realize there is nothing more artistic than to love others.—Vincent van Gogh

Whether your interest is Bach or bluegrass, arts or crafts, there are countless opportunities to either dress up or throw on a pair of jeans and head out to feed the eye, the mind, and the heart. There are symphony orchestras to tug at your heartstrings, folk-music festivals to get you dancing, and museums that showcase the magnificent craftsmanship of Kentucky quiltmakers (a double wedding band quilt might get your message across).

PERFORMANCE VENUES

The Kentucky Center for the Arts sparkles with excitement nearly every night of the year, offering a variety of music, large-scale Broadway theatrical productions, and dance performances. One of the nation's preeminent cultural venues, the Kentucky Center is home of the Lonesome Pine Series featuring indigenous music from around the world, the Midnight Ramble Series celebrating African-American arts, and the Bingham Series for classical music performances. The glass-arched lobby offers an amazing panoramic view of the Ohio River and the Falls Fountain. Before or after the show, stop by the on-site restaurant for dinner or drinks or marvel at the center's permanent collection of twentieth-century sculpture.

))))) **The Kentucky Center for the Arts**
Five Riverfront Plaza / Louisville / 502-562-0100

Featuring two concert halls, Lexington's main performance venue, the Singletary Center for the Arts, hosts everything from world-class symphonies to avant-garde dance to jazz. The Singletary Center is home to the Lexington Philharmonic, the University Artist Series, the Kentucky Artist Series, the Next Stage Series, and the Spotlight Jazz series, to name a few. There is almost always something going on here, and while you're waiting for the concert to begin you can ponder the Center's large-scale fiberworks or check out the latest temporary exhibit in the President's Room.

))))) **Singletary Center for the Arts**
     510 Rose Street / Lexington / 859-257-4942

The Lexington Opera House sets the mood for an evening of fine romance, as it is filled with plush red velvet, gold leaf, balconies, and even box seats (if you really want to impress your date). This is the stop for the *Broadway Live!* series, as well as the Kentucky Ballet Theatre.

))))) **Lexington Opera House**
     401 West Short Street / Lexington / 859-233-4567

Located in the peaceful setting of Centre College, the Norton Center for the Arts was designed by a member of the Frank Lloyd Wright Foundation. The center offers an impressive array of performances, including opera, theater, dance, Broadway shows, and some of the nation's best-known classical musicians.

))))) **Norton Center for the Arts**
     600 West Walnut Street / Danville / 877-448-7469

The magnificently restored Palace Theater plays host to a variety of musical acts, as well as a summer classic film series. The spectacular setting alone will ensure a memorable evening out. Opened in 1928 as a vaudeville house, the Palace has a hundred faces carved in the ceiling of its lobby, and the theater itself was designed to look like a village courtyard, complete with greenery and stars on the ceiling.

))))) **The Palace Theater**
625 South Fourth Avenue / Louisville / 502-583-4555

The Owensboro Symphony Orchestra calls RiverPark its home, and this is also the site of the International Bluegrass Music Museum. The center hosts a Broadway at RiverPark! series that boasts the most exciting shows from New York. The center offers a beautiful view of the river and perfectly sets the stage for an evening of magical entertainment.

RiverPark Center
101 Daviess Street / Owensboro / 270-687-2787

The Mountain Arts Center, or MAC, as it is affectionately known, hosts bluegrass and gospel concerts and monthly appearances by well-known country music artists. The center is also home to the US 23 Talent Showcase and the Kentucky Opry. The Opry blends country, bluegrass, oldies, and pop music with catchy lighting and a dash of mountain humor in a way that will have your toes tapping and your heart beating a little faster.

The Mountain Arts Center
Highway 114 / Prestonsburg / 888-622-2787
www.macarts.com

The building alone is worth the visit—the Capitol Arts Center is housed in a lavishly decorated 1939 Art Deco movie theater. The center offers a variety of concerts and events.

The Capitol Arts Center
416 East Main Street / Bowling Green / 270-782-2787

The Paramount Arts Center is also housed in a restored Art Deco movie palace (it was the first motion picture theater for "talkies" in the Ohio Valley). Featuring programs ranging from country to gospel to classical, the Paramount also hosts the Highway 23 Jamboree, a Grand Ole Opry-style show that encourages audience participation! If you want to impress your sweetheart in front of the whole world, try one of the open mic nights at the Friday coffeehouse.

Paramount Arts Center
1300 Winchester Avenue / Ashland / 606-234-3175

With offerings from ballet to *Brigadoon* to jazz to acrobats, you'll be able to impress your date with a dose of culture at the Lake Cumberland Performing Arts Series.

Lake Cumberland Performing Arts Series
Center Theater / Somerset / 606-677-6090

GREAT EXPECTATIONS: THEATER

The state is home to an impressive array of local and regional theater groups. So whether you're in the mood for comedy, a good cry, or a love story, you don't have to look far for a memorable—and romantic—evening at the theater.

The recipient of a Tony Award, the Actors Theatre is internationally recognized for its Humana Festival of New American Plays. For more than twenty years, the festival has featured plays, workshops, and exhibits that have turned the world's eye to Louisville. One of the nation's premiere regional theaters, the ATL houses three performance spaces under one roof and draws more than 200,000 patrons annually.

Actors Theatre of Louisville
316 West Main Street / Louisville / 800-4ATL-TIX

During June and July, watch some of your favorite musicals performed under the stars at Iroquois Park.

))))) **Music Theater Louisville**
   Iroquois Amphitheater / Louisville / 502-367-9493

Actors Guild presents a mix of new and celebrated plays in an intimate setting in downtown Lexington. The shop in the ground level of the theater features a marvelous collection of Kentucky crafts, including fiber art, pottery, wood crafts, and folk art.

))))) **Actors Guild of Lexington**
   139 West Short Street / Lexington 859-233-0663

The all-volunteer Studio Players is housed in a newly renovated building that was once the carriage house for the Bell House on stately Bell Court. The Studio Players offer a mixture of theater favorites and musicals that will make you yearn for a simpler time.

))))) **Studio Players**
   601-½ Sayre Avenue / Lexington
   859-254-8905

Under the stars in Louisville's Central Park, the romance of the Bard truly comes alive each summer at the Kentucky Shakespeare Festival. Now over forty years old, this is the oldest independent Shakespeare festival in North America—and most performances are free. Some of the greatest plays ever

---

highlight

"Stephen Foster"
The Musical

Each summer, audiences relive the early years of Stephen Foster, who according to legend penned "My Old Kentucky Home" while staying in Bardstown. In an outdoor setting, you can hum along to well-known songs such as "Beautiful Dreamer," watch live dances from the period, and relive the romance between Foster and his future wife in this colorful costume drama.

Stephen Foster: The Musical
Bardstown / 800-626-1563 /
www.stephenfoster.com

written come to life in a beautiful outdoor setting in a historic part of town. Make sure to arrive early so you have time to stroll St. James Court, taking in some truly stunning Victorian homes.

))))) **Kentucky Shakespeare Festival**
1114 South Third Street / Louisville / 502-583-8738
www.kyshakes.org

In the lovely setting of the arboretum, the Lexington Shakespeare Festival annually offers two Shakespeare and one other play each summer. With room for both chairs and blanket seating, the location is perfect for picnicking before the show or enjoying wine and dessert at intermission.

))))) **Lexington Shakespeare Festival**
University of Kentucky - Lexington-Fayette Urban County
Arboretum / 859-257-4929 / www.lexingtonshakespeare.org

Nestled in the scenic mountains of eastern Kentucky, the outdoor Jenny Wiley Theatre features musical and theatrical favorites during its summer seasons. With the sounds of crickets and whispering breezes as your background music, enjoy shows such as *Oklahoma!* and *South Pacific* under the twinkling stars.

▲ **Jenny Wiley Theatre**
Jenny Wiley State Resort Park / Prestonsburg
877-CALL-JWT

Having celebrated its fiftieth anniversary in 1999, the Pioneer Playhouse is a 1950s-style outdoor dinner theater that started the careers of actors such as Lee Majors and Jim Varney. During the summer season, the theater presents a mix of classics, comedies, and Tony Award winners. Before dinner and the show you can browse among the shops or stroll in the brick courtyard and enjoy the stars. There must be a lot of romance here—over thirty actors have married after meeting at the playhouse!

))))) **Pioneer Playhouse**
840 Stanford Road / Danville
859-236-2747

June through October, the Horse Cave Theater features a professional acting company offering performances of comedy, drama, classics, and original plays by Kentucky writers. Make it a weekend away at the theater—ask about the specials that include admission to three plays and overnight accommodations.

Horse Cave Theater
107 East Main Street / Horse Cave
1-800-342-2177
www.horsecavetheatre.org

There are many wonderful theaters and theater companies throughout the state. Following are just a few of the ones where you and your someone special are sure to find the perfect romantic setting.

))))) **Pine Knob Theatre**
Exit 95 at Wendell Ford Parkway
Leitchfield / 270-879-8190
www.pineknob.com

))))) **Bunbury Theatre**
112 South Seventh Street
Louisville / 502-585-5306

Theatre Workshop of Owensboro
407 West Fifth Street
Owensboro / 270-683-5333

Roadside Theater
91 Madison Avenue / Whitesburg / 606-633-0108

Village Players of Fort Thomas
8 North Fort Thomas Avenue / Fort Thomas / 859-781-3583

SHALL WE DANCE?

Whether you're interested in being an observer or a participant, few things offer more possibilities for romance than dance.

Enjoying an extremely loyal following, the Louisville Ballet attracts renowned national and international performers. For fifty seasons, the ballet has performed such favorites as *Swan Lake, Romeo and Juliet,* and *Cinderella.* What could be more romantic than dramatic lighting, gossamer costumes, and some of the world's greatest love stories set to beautiful music?

Louisville Ballet
315 East Main Street / Louisville / 502-583-3150

The Kentucky Ballet Theatre recognizes the romance inherent in dance—one of their recent performances was simply titled *Romantic Moods!* The company performs traditional and new works, with exciting offerings exploring Asian and Latin contributions to dance.

Ballet Under the Stars takes place annually at the first weekend of August at Woodland Park. This is a wonderful event that combines the inherent romantic nature of dance with a lovely outdoor setting.

Kentucky Ballet Theatre
736 National Avenue / Lexington / 859-252-5245

The Lexington Traditional Dance Association hosts contra dances, a form of traditional folk dance, several weekends a month, rotating between locations in Lexington, Louisville, and Berea. Live music will get you in the spirit of the evening, and often the dances are followed by impromptu gatherings for late-night swing dancing. An added bonus to the dances—because there's so much twirling involved, in order to keep from getting dizzy, it helps to gaze deeply into the eyes of your partner!

))))) **Lexington Traditional Dance Association**
Arts Place / Lexington / 859-389-7380

PLAYING YOUR HEARTSTRINGS: MUSICAL PERFORMANCES

Love is a friendship set to music.—*E. Joseph Cossman*

Kentuckians have a way with music. The state has been home to such greats as Rosemary Clooney, the Judds, and Loretta Lynn. Whether chamber music or a bluegrass band is more your style, it shouldn't take long to find a concert to tickle your musical fancy and set the stage for romance.

The Louisville Orchestra offers several series tailored to the musical interests of you and your special someone. Choose from the MasterWorks or Coffee Concerts (classical), SuperPops (popular music), NightLights (light classics), and the New Dimensions (contemporary music) series.

))))) **Louisville Orchestra**
611 West Main Street / Louisville / 502-584-7777

The Louisville Chorus is the oldest of the choral groups in Louisville and performs a wide variety of music. Make sure you don't miss their annual Valentine's dinner and concert.

))))) **Louisville Chorus**
204 Breckinridge Lane / Louisville / 502-895-7070

The Lexington Philharmonic's variety of series will have something for everyone, whether you love the classics, the more casual setting of the Pops Series, or the intimate settings of the Coffee Series. While the regular series performances at the Singletary Center make a wonderful date, the most romantic thing the Philharmonic puts on is the annual Picnic with the Pops, held in August at the Kentucky Horse Park. Tables of eight are decorated in themes, and you'll see everything from red roses and tuxedos to people dressed as astronauts. Even the least expensive seats—blanket seating—make for a special evening under the stars. Towards the end of the concert, the orchestra performs a waltz and encourages everyone to get up and dance!

))))) **Lexington Philharmonic Orchestra**
Lexington / 859-233-4226

Originally built in 1932 as a vaudeville house, the Sipp Theatre was renovated in the 1990s and now hosts fifteen concerts a year. Performances range from concerts given by the Lexington Philharmonic to the "Bluegrass at the Sipp" series.

The Historic Sipp Theatre
Paintsville / 606-789-9014

Try impressing your date by attending the recording of a radio show that will be broadcast by more than 160 stations. Musicians and songwriters from all over the world perform a wide variety of music at the Monday night concerts in the Woodsongs series. Sitting in on the recording sessions have become a popular outing, so make your reservations early.

))))) **Woodsongs**
The Kentucky Theatre / Lexington
859-231-6997

On Tuesday nights from May through August, you can bring a lawn chair and enjoy the sounds of live jazz, blues, and big band music at Jazz & Blues in the Great Outdoors.

))))) **Jazz & Blues in the Great Outdoors**
Lexington / 859-288-2900

The Troubadour Concert Series features ten concerts a year, held at the Kentucky Theatre in Lexington on Thursdays and then moving to the Paramount Arts Center in Ashland for a Friday concert. The series has featured such artists as Bruce Hornsby, Nanci Griffith, and Hank Williams, Jr.

The Troubadour Concert Series
Lexington / 859-231-6997 / Ashland / 606-324-3175

Since 1939, the Renfro Valley Entertainment Center has hosted twelve shows a week featuring its own resident troupe as well as headliner concerts. Home of the Renfro Valley Barn Dance, the center offers traditional folk music, gospel, and contemporary country. The Country Music Store comes complete with rockers and a checkerboard, so you can stop and sit a spell. Or, visit the six-pew Freedom Church, the site of several recent weddings. If you're here in late June, be sure to stay for the Old Joe Clark Bluegrass Festival, where some of the state's best pickers and singers will perform traditional music.

Renfro Valley Entertainment Center
Renfro Valley / 800-765-7464

This 40-year-old subscription series presents classical, choral, and dance performances at venues in London, Corbin, Barbourville, and Williamsburg.

The Fine Arts Association of
Southeastern Kentucky, Inc.
1102 Pine Street / Corbin
606-528-4824

In addition to these regular concerts, there are an amazing number of music festivals throughout the state. Anytime between April and October, you can sit with your sweetheart and enjoy the sounds of blues and barbershop, fiddles and dulcimers. Following are only a few of the many musical offerings out there—check the local newspaper or

highlight

Strike Up the Band

The college town of Danville springs into a pleasant bustle of activity each summer as it plays host to the internationally recognized Great American Brass Band Festival. The festivities begin with a turn-of-the-century tea and Chautauqua performance and are followed by a balloon race, parade, picnic, Sunday morning worship service, and concerts. Tens of thousands of people gather in Danville to hear the whole spectrum of brass bands, including Civil War, ragtime, circus, and traditional brass band music performed by groups from all over the world. If this event doesn't get your heart going, what else will?

Great American Brass Band
Festival
Centre College Campus
Danville / 859-236-7794

with the Kentucky Department of Tourism for a complete listing.

The Kentucky Opry
Mountain Arts Center / Prestonsburg / 888-622-2787

Celebration of Traditional Music
Berea / 859-986-9341 (ext. 5140)

Yellowbanks Dulcimer Festival
Owensboro / 800-489-1131

Festival of the Bluegrass
Lexington / 859-846-4995

Singing under the Stars Gospel Festival
Russell Springs / 270-866-7370

Kentucky Shaker Music Weekend
Pleasant Hill, Harrodsburg / 800-734-5611

Official Kentucky State Championship Old Time Fiddler's Contest
Falls of Rough / 270-259-3578

Poppy Mountain Bluegrass Festival
Morehead / 606-784-2277

MUSEUMS

A museum outing is a wonderful way to get to know someone or to get re-acquainted with someone you thought you already knew everything about. Looking at art can be a very personal and emotional experience, putting you in touch with beauty, the body's form, and the joy and complexity of everyday experience. From collections of paintings and sculpture to quilts and exquisite handmade crafts, Kentucky's museums will give you something to talk about and wonderful things to discover together.

The state's first art museum, the Speed Art Museum has a collection that covers over 6,000 years of human creation. Recently renovated, the museum has added many new pieces to its collection, which includes gothic altarpieces and sculpture as well as works by masters such as Monet, Rembrandt, and Picasso. If your tastes are a bit more modern, the Speed also offers modern American, African, and Native-American art. The museum is often a stop for important traveling exhibits, so there's always something new to see.

))))) **The Speed Art Museum**
2035 South Third Street / Louisville / 502-634-2700

The University of Kentucky's Art Museum houses a permanent collection of nearly 4,000 European and American paintings, sculptures, prints, drawings, photographs, and decorative arts. From the folk art of the self-taught Edgar Tolson to the luminous light in the paintings of the baroque Italian painter Carracci, the pieces in this gallery's inviting space will give you a new perspective on the beauty of love and life.

))))) **University of Kentucky Art Museum**
Rose Street and Euclid Avenue / Lexington / 859-257-5716

The Headley-Whitney Museum has a wonderful collection in decorative arts, with a special focus on jewelry and bibelots. Perhaps most unusual is the museum's shell grotto, where you'll find yourself in a room whose walls are decorated with luminous, colorful shells.

))))) **Headley-Whitney Museum**
4435 Old Frankfort Pike / Lexington / 859-255-6653

In addition to works by Edgar Degas and Sir Thomas Lawrence, the Owensboro Museum of Fine Art has developed a strong collection of works by Kentucky artists from the 1800s to the present. Worth a special visit are the sixteen turn-of-the-century stained-glass windows reaching twenty-five feet into the air. The museum's support organization also organizes special events during the year, such as Omnicraft, a festival of Kentucky artists and craftsmen.

Owensboro Museum of Fine Art
901 Frederica Street / Owensboro / 270-685-3181

One of the jewels of downtown Paducah, the Market House Museum preserves local history. Make sure to see the complete interior of an 1877 drugstore! The Yeiser specializes in the visual arts and fine crafts from this region as well as from around the world. Their permanent collection and traveling exhibits range from the historic to the contemporary.

Market House Museum and Yeiser Art Center
200 Broadway / Paducah / 502-443-7759; 502-442-2453

The diverse collection in the Kentucky Museum has something for everyone. Whether you're interested in American or European paintings, decorative arts, or Shaker art and history, you're sure to find something that will excite the mind and get you talking.

The Kentucky Museum
Western Kentucky University / Bowling Green / 270-745-6258

John James Audubon was one of the world's most celebrated nature artists, focusing his talent on the study of birds. The museum which bears his name showcases not only his work but has exhibits on plants and natural history. You can probably even find a moment alone in the nature observatory.

John James Audubon Museum
Hwy. 421 North / Henderson / 270-827-1893

Each June, the Folk Art Center hosts a week-long Appalachian Celebration recognizing Kentucky's rich mountain heritage in music, dance, crafts, storytelling, and folk art.

Kentucky Folk Art Center
102 West First Street / Morehead / 606-783-2204

If not the site for blockbuster exhibits, smaller and speciality museums can still be the locale for love. Feel free to stroll in the quiet and solitude in the following smaller exhibit spaces.

Allen R. Hite Art Institute
University of Louisville, Belknap Campus / Louisville
502-852-6794

Berea College Museum
103 Jackson Street / Berea / 859-986-9341 #6078

Eagle Gallery, Murray State University
Fifteenth and Olive Streets / Murray / 270-762-3052

HANDS-ON ARTS

Indulge your creativity as you paint mugs, plates, and picture frames. Create and design pottery and ceramic giftware—for yourself or your sweetheart—and the store will fire it for you.

Paint Spot
4600 Shelbyville Road / Louisville / 502-899-7768

Sometimes making art together leads to a declaration of love: we know of at least one proposal that occurred while a local couple was painting at the Mad Potter.

The Mad Potter
3385 Tates Creek Road / Lexington / 859-269-4591.

)))) **Brush Fire! At Colonial Garden Center**
   4432 Old Nicholasville Road / Lexington / 859-272-6698

The contemporary visual arts center operated by the Louisville Visual Arts Association offers exhibits and art sales at the Water Tower, a National Historic Landmark located on the Ohio River; gallery and studio tours; special events; and the Louisville Film & Video Festival. Artopia Creative Arts Studios is an educational facility offering classes on everything from jewelry making and ceramics to screenwriting and decorative paper and bookmaking.

)))) **Louisville Visual Art Association**
   3500 River Road / Louisville
   502-895-3700 / www.louisvillevisualart.org

All the
Right
Moves

To love and win is the best thing; to love and lose, the next best.

—*William Makepeace Thackeray*

Sporting events and related activities may not be your first idea for a romantic outing, but here in the state where many people proudly bleed the royal blue of University of Kentucky sports, such things are serious business indeed.

Beyond the ever-popular basketball and football, Kentucky also offers endless activities for horse lovers, whether you're more interested in being an observer or participant. You can get gussied up and spend the afternoon at a steeplechase or throw on jeans and enjoy the wonders of nature from atop a horse on a trail ride.

If water is more your thing, the state has nearly endless opportunities for recreation. Home to fourteen major river systems, Kentucky is a place where you can while away the afternoon on a quiet canoe ride or get your heart racing as you brave the rapids.

ALL THE PRETTY HORSES:
FARM TOURS AND EVENTS

The Bluegrass region is a bit like Hollywood in that visitors often ask where they can see the homes of celebrities. The only difference is that in Kentucky, champion thoroughbreds are the celebrities, and their homes are magnificent barns surrounded by miles of bluegrass farmland and white fences. These are the quintessential images of the central part of the state. And for good reason—they inspire us with the inherent romance associated with horses.

Fourteen Kentucky Derby winners since 1976 have been retired to the Lexington area, and many of their farms are open to the public. Although many horse-farm tours are free, it is customary to tip the groom who shows you around.

Gainesway Farm is home of 1988 Derby-winner Winning Colors. Call to make a free appointment, but note that seeing Winning Colors is not part of the tour.

))))) **Gainesway Farm**
   3750 Paris Pike / Lexington
   859-293-2676

Owned by William Farish, who hosts former President George Bush and Queen Elizabeth II when they visit the races, Lane's End is home to 1999 Derby-winner Charismatic.

))))) **Lane's End Farm**
   1500 Midway Road / Versailles
   859-873-7300

Three Chimneys Farm is home to 1977 Triple Crown-winner Seattle Slew and 1997 Derby-winner Silver Charm.

))))) **Three Chimneys Farm**
   1981 Old Frankfort Pike / Midway
   859-873-7053

Located near Lexington's Bluegrass airport and the Keeneland Race Track, Jonabell Farm is the final resting place for Affirmed, who with jockey (and Walton, Kentucky native) Steve Cauthen won the Triple Crown in 1978, the last time this feat was accomplished. There are no public tours of Jonabell, but free showings of the stallions, are available at 1 P.M. Monday through Friday. No need to call in advance for visits.

))))) **Jonabell Farm**
3333 Bowman Mill Road / Lexington / 859-255-8537

Enjoy a free tour led by a fifty-year employee of this storied farm. Calumet Farm's signature red-and-white buildings are among the most-recognized sights in the state. Tour highlights include a visit to the Calumet cemetery, the final resting place for racing greats Citation, Alydar, Whirlaway, and Bull Lea. To complete the tour, we recommend a stop at the Kentucky Horse Park for a viewing of the farm's collection of racing trophies.

))))) **Calumet Farm**
3301 Versailles Road / Lexington / 859-231-8272

A guided tour of famed Claiborne Farm includes a visit to the tombstone marking the grave of Secretariat, the 1973 Triple Crown winner considered by many to be the greatest race horse of all time. Visiting hours are limited. Phone ahead for a free tour by the grooms.

))))) **Claiborne Farm**
703 Winchester Road / Paris / 859-233-4252

Farm tours are a great way to understand what makes the horse industry so special—and a wonderful excuse for a beautiful drive in the country. To arrange tours of other historic farms, contact one of the following agencies.

))))) **Historic and Horse Farm Tours / Lexington / 859-268-2906**

))))) **Blue Grass Tours / Lexington / 859-252-5744**

))))) **Kentucky Horse Tours / 800-873-7889**

The eyes of the world turn to the graceful twin spires at Churchill Downs annually for the two most exciting minutes in sports. If you're lucky enough to get tickets, dress to the nines and make sure to find a special hat. Even if you don't go to the race, Louisville puts on quite a show in the weeks preceding the Derby. From headliner concerts to art shows to the Thunder Over Louisville fireworks extravaganza, there's no excuse not to grab your sweetheart and join in the fun.

))))) **Churchill Downs**
700 Central Avenue / Louisville / 800-283-3729

With meets in April and October, excitement, tradition, and a beautiful setting combine to make an afternoon at Keeneland Race Course a memorable event. Stroll near the paddock to pick your favorite for the next race. Or, if you're in the mood for a moment at Keeneland away from the crowds, go to watch the early-morning workouts. After the breathtaking sight of the horses racing through the morning mists, you and your special someone can enjoy breakfast at the track kitchen.

))))) **Keeneland Race Course**
4201 Versailles Road / Lexington / 800-456-3412

Who wouldn't love this impressive 1,032-acre park dedicated to our passion for horses? You can admire the Parade of Breeds, trace equine history at the International Museum of the Horse, or see Derby winner Pleasant Colony (1981). A walking tour will let you see the park at your own speed, with plenty of time for admiring the beauty of the park's setting and the majesty of the horses. Perhaps even more romantic, take a ride in a covered wagon or surrey, or contact the park to find out the dates of the summer carriage driving weekend. The Horse Park also offers guided trail rides.

))))) **Kentucky Horse Park**
4089 Iron Works Pike / Lexington
859-233-4303

Each of the following three events is held annually at the Kentucky Horse Park, and they all hold their own special charm.

The Three-Day Event is designed to measure the athletic ability of both horse and rider in elegant dressage, a challenging cross-country course, and stadium jumping.

The High Hope Steeplechase cries out for a picnic to celebrate the immense beauty of the bluegrass in May. Whether you're dressed up and having a catered affair or tailgating with a bucket of fried chicken, a day of sun, horses, and food and drink is a wonderful way to celebrate your togetherness.

Legend has it that women have fallen in love after staring into the deep, soulful eyes of the Arabian horse. The Egyptian Event will give you the chance to test that

---

highlight

Happy Trails
DH Resorts

If you really want to get cozy with your horse and your mate, DH Resorts is the place for you. To get closer to nature, the Western Village offers secluded cabins and horse camping. The Mountain Lake Manor provides large private rooms with a few more creature comforts. DH Resorts offers a wide variety of programs, including open and private trail rides, lunch rides, and overnight rides where you grill your dinner under the stars. Bonfires, hayrides, canoeing, and a country barn dance are all available—and they will even help coordinate your wedding.

Western Village
Route 1 / Hillsboro
800-737-RIDE

theory. The event features the Showcase of Stallions, barn parties, and a bazaar displaying art and traditional costumes.

))))) **Rolex Kentucky Three-Day Event / 859-233-2362**

))))) **High Hope Steeplechase / 859-255-5727**

))))) **The Pyramid Society's Annual Egyptian Event / 859-231-0771**

If you prefer trotters and pacers, the Red Mile is the place for your evening out. With meets in spring and fall, the Red Mile also features clubhouse dining with a view of the track and downtown.

))))) **Red Mile Harness Track**
1200 Red Mile Road / Lexington
859-255-0752

The world's largest outdoor horse show, the Junior League Horse Show is a great way to spend an evening in July. You can marvel at the form of horses in the three- and five-gaited classes, root for your favorite horse in the roadster class, and admire the precision of the hackney ponies. Even if you don't know anything about show horses, you and your date can pick your favorite fabulously elaborate name, watch the flying formal wear, and enjoy the view as the sun slips behind the Lexington skyline.

))))) **Lexington Junior League Horse Show**
Red Mile Harness Track / Lexington / 859-252-1893

RIDING INTO THE SUNSET

For good reason, Kentucky is known as the horse capital of the world. So why not try a trail ride with your sweetheart? Six of the state parks (Kentucky Dam Village, Lake Barkley, Barren River Lake, Lake Cumberland, Carter Caves, and Cumberland Falls) have stables on site. Iroquois Park in Louisville offers trail rides, and you'll find private stables dotted across the Commonwealth.

Located near Hopkinsville, Copper Canyon Ranch stable offers rides through scenic backwoods and through a recreated 1800s mining town. Primitive camping is available here, and they even host weddings!

Copper Canyon Ranch / 270-269-2416

There are plenty of stables that arrange for short and long trail rides. Following are some of our favorites:

Iroquois Stable
Louisville / 502-363-9159

Big Red Stables
1605 Jackson Pike / Harrodsburg / 859-734-3118

Shady Creek Riding Stable
Eddyville / 270-388-5365

Deer Run Stables
2001 River Circle Drive / Richmond / 859-527-6339

Wildwood Stables
Nicholasville / 859-885-9359

Jesse James Riding Stable
Cave City / 502-773-2560

THE BIG SCORE: BASKETBALL AND FOOTBALL

College sports can be a real factor in a relationship. After all, it is important to make sure your significant other is not a closet fan of a Southeastern Conference team you despise. If both partners are willing participants, getting swept up in the excitement and the adrenaline of a close basketball or football game can be a great way to spend time with someone special. And now that women's teams are becoming more competitive, it's even easier to experience the thrill of sport.

Depending on how the season is going, the Cats or Cards may be the main thing on your honey's mind during March. Since you can't fight the madness, you might as well join in the fun.

))))) **University of Kentucky Wildcat Basketball**
   Rupp Arena / Lexington
   859-257-1818

))))) **University of Louisville Cardinal Basketball**
   Freedom Hall / Louisville
   502-852-5151

Though a huge football stadium might not be the most intimate of places, pre-game tailgating with a special meal for two is a great way to start the festivities. And if a cold snap hits, try heating things up by taking a thermos of hot cocoa and a blanket big enough for two.

))))) **University of Kentucky Wildcat Football**
   Commonwealth Stadium
   Lexington / 859-257-1818

))))) **University of Louisville Cardinal Football**
   Papa John's Cardinal Stadium
   Louisville / 502-852-5151

Love Field: AAA Baseball

Admit it—ever since you saw the movie *Bull Durham* (in which Susan Sarandon and Kevin Costner prove that love, lust, and sports *do* mix), minor league baseball has seemed filled with romantic promise. Even if you're not a big baseball fan, it's hard to go wrong with cold beer, ballpark hot dogs, green grass, and summer breezes. The Riverbats' new stadium offers a great view of the city skyline, and the park is even equipped with a twenty-two-horse carousel. Lexington has also started its own AAA team, and the park comes complete with a restaurant and picnic area.

))))) **Lexington Legends**
1245 North Broadway / Lexington / 859-252-4487

))))) **Louisville Riverbats**
Louisville Slugger Field / Louisville / 502-367-9121

While you've got baseball on the brain, check out the Louisville Slugger Museum, where you can watch the famous wooden bats being made and see the world's largest bat and fielder's mitt.

))))) **Louisville Slugger Museum**
800 West Main Street / Louisville / 502-588-7228

Biking

Biking is another wonderful way to enjoy nature and one another. The Department of Tourism offers a great booklet called *Kentucky Bicycle Tours* (**800-225-8747**), which will give you specific directions, the history of the areas you'll be riding through, and even the location of the nearest bike shop.

From April through October, cycling events are happening in various parts of the state. Why not try the Tour de Heart (a two-day benefit ride between Louisville and Carrollton) or the Horsey Hundred (a route beginning in Georgetown and winding through scenic horse country)?

A RIVER RUNS THROUGH IT:
CANOEING AND RAFTING

The course of true love never did run smooth.—William Shakespeare

Canoeing and rafting outings let you and your special someone work and play together. You can enjoy a sedate ride down a gently flowing stream or experience the heart-stopping excitement of rafting whitewater on a mountain river. Kentucky has a number of rivers that are classified as wild rivers, meaning that they are free flowing and have undeveloped natural shorelines. The lower Rockcastle River is a top spot for whitewater canoeing, and the Cumberland River, the Red River, and the Green River all offer magnificent scenery. The following companies offer rafting and canoe trips in various parts of the state:

)))) **Sheltowee Trace Outfitters / 800-541-7238**

)))) **Canoe Kentucky / 800-K-CANOE-1**

)))) **Elkhorn Adventures Whitewater Rafting / 859-754-5080**

---

highlight

Right Up Your Alley!

If love in the lanes turns you on, there's probably not a more romantic place to bowl than Vernon Lanes. Located in a turn-of-the-century Italianate house, Vernon Lanes was originally the home of a men's recreational club. But in 1946, someone wisely decided that it was time to let the ladies in, and the rest, as they say, is history.

Vernon Lanes
1575 Story Avenue
Louisville
502-584-8460

Float in a canoe by scenic farmland in northern Kentucky or camp overnight by the Licking River's edge.

))))) **Licking River Canoe Rental**
859-472-2000

In addition to scenic day trips, Barren River Canoe Rentals offers canoe camping at Mammoth Cave National Park.

Barren River Canoe Rentals
270-796-1979

Mountain Wander Kayaks organizes both touring trips and white-water kayak trips.

Mountain Wander Kayaks
270-428-4690

In addition to offering leisurely trips on Elkhorn Creek and the Kentucky River, Still Waters Canoe Trails conducts romantic "moonlight floats." From May to October on full-moon weekends, guides will take you and your sweetheart out among the sparkling shadows on the waters of the Kentucky. And at the end of the trip, they serve dinner and let you roast marshmallows around a roaring campfire.

))))) **Still Waters Canoe Trails**
Frankfort / 502-223-8896

Appendix: Further Resources

www.kentucky.com
A great source for basic information about entertainment, restaurants, lodging, and other state offerings.

Kentucky's Bed & Breakfast Guide
www.bbonline.com/ky/bbak
This annual color guide is published by the Bed and Breakfast Association of Kentucky.

Kentucky Department of Fish and Wildlife
#1 Game Farm Road / Frankfort / 800-858-1549
www.state.ky.us/agencies/fw

The Kentucky Department of Travel
P. O. Box 2011 / Frankfort / 800-225-TRIP
www.kentuckytourism.com
Publisher of the excellent *Great Getaway Guide*. The Department of Travel is also a partner in the privately published *Kentucky Travel Guide*, an annual guide to events and places of interest throughout the Commonwealth. Both publications are free for the asking and are available at tourist and visitor centers statewide.

Kentucky Travel Guide
812 South Third Street / Louisville / 502-584-2722
www.kytravel.com

Kentucky State Parks
800-255-PARK / www.kystateparks.com

Kentucky Monthly Magazine
213 Clair Street / Frankfort / 888-329-0053
www.kentuckymonthly.com

Louisville Magazine
137 West Muhammad Ali Boulevard / Louisville / 502-625-0100
www.louisville.com/loumag

LEO: Louisville Eccentric Observer
600 E. Main Street, #102 / Louisville / 502-895-9770
www.louisville.com/leo.html

ACE Weekly
486 West Second Street / Lexington / 859-225-4889
www.acemagazine.com
Louisville and Lexington both have outstanding alternative maga-
zines available at no cost at local restaurants, bookstores, libraries,
and other public locales.

Arts Across Kentucky
2891 Richmond Road, Suite 103 / Lexington / 859-266-4888
This magazine covers the state's art, crafts, travel, and entertainment
industries.

Lexington Herald-Leader
100 Midland Avenue / Lexington / 859-253-1314; 800-999-8881
www.kentuckyconnect.com/heraldleader

Louisville Courier-Journal
525 West Broadway / P. O. Box 740031 / Louisville / 502-582-4011
www.courier-journal.com

University Press of Kentucky
663 Limestone Street / Lexington / 859-257-5200
www.kentuckypress.com
Publisher of great books about Kentucky history, literature, culture, people, and geography.

Cincinnati Magazine
705 Central Avenue / Suite 370 / Cincinnati / 513-421-4300

Cincinnati Enquirer
312 Elm Street / Cincinnati / 513-721-2700
www.enquirer.com/today/
Cincinnati Magazine and the *Cincinnati Enquirer* frequently cover Kentucky getaways and restaurant reviews, particularly from the northern part of the state.

Back Home in Kentucky
295 Old Forge Mill Road / Clay City / 800-264-5899

Kentucky Living Magazine
PO Box 32171 / Louisville / 800-KY-LIVING
www.kentuckyliving.com
This monthly offers wonderful, comprehensive listings of arts activities, historic tours, and fairs and festivals.

Kentucky Educational Television
600 Cooper Drive / Lexington / 859-258-7000 / www.KET.org
Kentucky Educational Television, or KET, broadcasts locally produced news programs, documentaries, and arts and culture offerings on the Bluegrass State through its network of stations across the state.

Index